MOMENTS WITH GOD

Georgette Butcher, an Anglican, was for many years Manager of London's leading branch of the Scripture Union bookshops, until her formal retirement in 1982.

She is now Editor of the influential magazine, *The Christian Bookseller*.

GEORGETTE BUTCHER

Moments With God

Collins
FOUNT PAPERBACKS

First published by Fount Paperbacks, London in 1984

© Georgette Butcher 1984

Made and printed in Great Britain by
William Collins Sons & Co Ltd, Glasgow

Contents

Introduction

This book is intended for those who want to take a few moments in a busy day to be quiet and to take time with God.

Each reading is in four parts. First, a few verses from the Bible can be meditated upon briefly, or for longer if time allows. By doing this we can draw our minds away from whatever has been occupying them, from the busy thoughts and cares that crowd in, and dwell on our God.

Each passage of Scripture is followed by a short related reading from the work of a Christian writer. Some of these passages are practical, others can teach us or are more devotional. The final prayer should lead into personal prayer which will naturally follow the way that we have been led by the reading.

The sections follow the pattern of a day, which from its dawn to its close is also an echo of our life. Any of the sections can, of course, be read at any time. I have written in the hope that each reader may find something that will come as a message of strength and comfort for the hour, but that will also remain with her. We all need this message, and God so often supplies that need through Christian writers and their books. Such books have been a part of my life for a long time; I am grateful to the writers who have given so much to me, and happy to share their gift, along with that of the most precious book of all, with all who read *Moments With God*. Any passages which are not ascribed to other authors are my own.

January 1984   Georgette Butcher

As the Day Begins
In Your Hands, Lord

Praise the Lord, O my soul; all my inmost being, praise his holy name. Psalm 103:1

Very early in the morning, while it was still dark, Jesus got up, left the house and went off to a solitary place, where he prayed. Mark 1:35

For many of us a solitary place may be at the kitchen table, in bed with a cup of tea before rising, or on the bus or train on the way to work. If, however, we are determined to spend time with God that place where we meet with him can become hallowed ground. It is here that for a little time our whole being is concentrated on our Lord and we can praise him and thank him for his gifts as well as commit the day to him, not only for ourselves but for those we love and those for whom we have a concern.

This time that is spent with God is utterly personal, and we meet him within ourselves. Our acknowledgement of his presence can be without words as we relax in the surety of his love and ponder on his greatness. When we do move on to using words we lay our needs before him, and not only our own needs but the needs of the world. The world is his and because of his concern we should also be concerned. God wants to help us in the living of each day, but he also wants our prayers to help bring about his will for all his created beings.

I commit this day to you, thanking you for your love.
Help me to be faithful in my work and to do it remembering
always that you are with me. Make me conscious of your
people and that the world, with all its nations, belongs to
you. I pray that your purposes may be fulfilled everywhere.

*

Sing to the Lord, for he has done glorious things. Isaiah
12:5

In my Father's house are many rooms; if it were not so, I
would have told you. I am going there to prepare a place for
you . . . I will come back and take you to be with me that
you also may be where I am. John 14:2–3

The fact that the Lord is coming is a far more important
issue than questions of when it will all take place, or the
precise nature of the events which will accompany his coming. He is coming – *that* is the great reality; exactly when
and precisely how, though important in their way, are in the
end secondary issues. Christ is coming, he is destined to
reign in his eternal glory and to inherit the glory and honour
of heaven and earth. That and nothing else is the substance
of the Christian hope, and that is the centre around which
all other aspects of the Last Things find their proper place.

Bruce Milne, *The End of the World*

I would like to live my life in the light of your coming again, Lord – ready in every way and always expectant.

*

Serve the Lord with gladness; come before him with joyful songs. Psalm 100:2

On the last and greatest day of the Feast, Jesus stood and said in a loud voice, 'If a man is thirsty, let him come to me and drink. Whoever believes in me, as the Scripture has said, streams of living water will flow from within him.' By this he meant the Spirit, whom those who believed in him were later to receive. Up to that time the Spirit had not been given, since Jesus had not yet been glorified. John 7:37–39

We should make a deliberate effort at the outset of every day to recognize the person of the Holy Spirit, to move into the light concerning his presence in our consciousness and to open up our minds and to share all our thoughts and plans as we gaze by faith into the face of God. We should continue to walk throughout the day in a relationship of communication and communion with the Spirit, mediated through our knowledge of the Word, relying upon every office of the Holy Spirit's role as Counsellor mentioned in Scripture. We should acknowledge him as the illumination of truth and of the glory of Christ. We should look to him as teacher, guide, sanctifier, giver of assurance concerning our sonship and standing before God, helper in prayer, and as the one who directs and empowers witness. When this

practice of the presence of God is maintained over a period
of time, our experience of the Holy Spirit becomes less
subjective and more clearly identifiable as gradually we
learn to distinguish the strivings of the Spirit from the
motions of our flesh.

Richard F. Lovelace, *Dynamics of Spiritual Life*

Father, I pray that I may be steadfast in my commitment to
you. Help me by your Spirit to be faithful, to walk with you
in every aspect of my life, so that I may really please you and
you may be able to work through me. Help me to live so
that other people see you in me; but keep me utterly unself-
conscious, a channel for the Holy Spirit.

*

I will sing of the love of the Lord for ever. Psalm 89:1

The next day Jesus decided to leave for Galilee. Finding
Philip, he said to him, 'Follow me.' John 1:43

The most basic term we use for the Christian life is a term of
movement. We talk about following Jesus! And that implies
a refusal to stand still, we stick with him, we follow him,
even when he does not tell us exactly where he is taking us
or how we are going to get there. Living in hope is a life of
adventure, of openness to the future with all its hidden
possibilities. I do not think the subject of God's guidance
for our lives is an easy one to handle. There do not seem to
be any clearcut rules by which to work things out. But if

there are any rules, one of the most basic ones is that we should be ready for surprises!

Stephen H. Travers,
I Believe in the Second Coming of Christ

Give me the courage, I pray, to look on my life with you as an adventure; keep me moving forward eagerly, that I may be continually learning the lessons of faith and trust.

*

There is no one holy like the Lord. 1 Samuel 2:2

In the beginning was the Word, and the Word was with God, and the Word was God. He was with God in the beginning. Through him all things were made; without him nothing was made that has been made. In him was life, and that life was the light of men. John 1:1–2

> Jesus is the name we worship,
> Jesus is the Friend we love,
> Jesus is our Lord and Saviour,
> King of Heaven above.
>
> Jesus knows when we are troubled,
> Jesus hears our every prayer,
> Jesus has our trials and sorrows
> Always in his care.

Jesus made the lame go walking,
Jesus made the blind to see,
Jesus healed the sick and wounded:
Wondrous, O was he!

Jesus is our great redeemer,
Jesus died for you and me,
Jesus took our sins and failings,
Bore them on the Tree.

Jesus lives within us daily,
Jesus in our hearts will stay
Till we meet with him in heaven
On that glorious day.

Alan Durden, *Jesus Praise*

I humbly offer you my praise and worship, lost in the wonder of all that you are, and all that you have accomplished. In you is all that I can ever need – thank you for the gift of yourself.

*

I will praise God's name in song and glorify him with thanksgiving. Psalm 69:30

He guides me in paths of righteousness for his name's sake. Even though I walk through the valley of the shadow of death, I will fear no evil, for you are with me; your rod and staff, they comfort me. Psalm 23:3–4

It has become obvious that the problem of evil in the face of a loving God is not to be solved at a purely intellectual level. The human mind, in grappling with this enigma, brings God down to its own level, thereby degrading him and obscuring its own sight. On the contrary, it is by traversing the valley where death casts its long shadow that the sufferer learns basic truths about this condition. If he has the courage and the faith to proceed along the perilous path of self-discovery he will come to the other side of life a changed person who knows God rather than merely believes in him.

Martin Israel, *The Pain that Heals*

The valleys are dark places, Lord, and I am often fearful. Grant me a trusting, obedient heart that follows the Shepherd closely.

*

I will praise you, O Lord, with all my heart. Psalm 9:1

The Lord had said to Abram, 'Leave your country, your people and your father's household and go to the land I will show you. I will make you into a great nation and I will bless you; I will make your name great, and you will be a blessing.' Genesis 12:1–2

The more one surrenders to God, the more trouble does one take to find out what he wants, studying the Scriptures so as to get to know him better, listening for his voice in prayer, and being more severe than ever with oneself in one's efforts to track down the sin that makes us impermeable to his inspiration. But the whole atmosphere in which one does these things is new. It is an atmosphere, in fact, of adventure. It is the adventure of faith, exciting, difficult and exacting, but full of poetry, of new discoveries, of fresh turns and sudden surprises. It is adventure with God, a daily adventure, which does not belong only to a few exceptional pious times but to every minute affecting every thought, every feeling and every act. . . .

Uncertainty, doubts and hesitations remain, but now we can take them all to God and ask him to reveal himself and his designs to us. Instead of looking on our personal problems as annoying vexations we find that they provide a vital stimulus, a factor of new growth, transforming our personality and opening up new horizons and richer adventures for us. . . .

Our attitude to life is always a reflection of our attitude to God. Saying 'Yes' to God is saying 'Yes' to life, to all its problems and difficulties – 'Yes' instead of 'No', an attitude of adventure instead of one of going on strike. In such an adventure we commit our whole being.

Paul Tournier, *The Adventure of Living*

Father, give to me the faith that steps out into each day looking for adventure with you.

*

The Lord is my rock, my fortress and my deliverer.
2 Samuel 22:2

Jesus went up into the hills and called to him those he wanted, and they came to him. He appointed twelve – designating them apostles – that they might be with him and that he might send them out to preach and to have authority to drive out demons. Mark 3:13–14

When Jesus walking by the Lake of Galilee saw two brothers, Simon and Andrew, and challenged them to follow him, he received from them a personal response. 'They left their nets and followed him.' They certainly did not know all there was to know about him. Though they may have actually mixed with him from boyhood, they had only begun to glimpse the significance of that astonishing young man who so imperiously, and yet so lovingly, summoned them. But they knew enough to venture to respond, to follow, even though the way ahead was mysteriously dark. And when they said 'Yes' to him, responding with all they knew of themselves to all that they knew of him, they began a relationship with that 'wonderful counsellor' which was capable of almost infinite development. Their need was met by his mercy, their weakness by his strength, their ignorance by his wisdom. They began to know him 'whom to know is life eternal'.

Donald Coggan, *Convictions*

Thank you for your call to us to follow you. Help all those who find it difficult to respond.

*

Rejoice in the Lord always. Philippians 4:4

– an angel of the Lord appeared to him in a dream and said,
'Joseph son of David, do not be afraid to take Mary home as
your wife, because what is conceived in her is from the Holy
Spirit. She will give birth to a son, and you are to give him
the name Jesus, because he will save his people from their
sins.' Matthew 1:20–21

The Hebrews attached great significance to choosing a name
for a newborn child. The name often indicated the role the
child was to play in the family or in the history of the
people. The son of Isaiah the prophet, for example, was
named 'Shear-Jashub', 'A remnant will return'. And the
very name symbolized the people who, after Isaiah's own
time, would return from exile and punishment. Later, John
the Baptist was named at God's command, contrary to the
inclination of his relatives, as a sign that the child's life was
more than ordinary, that he was especially chosen from the
moment of birth to play a unique role in the plan of salvation.

Little wonder, then, that when God came to dwell among
us he chose a name that would indicate who he was and
what his mission would be. Now, the word 'Jesus or
Yeshua' in Aramaic means 'Yahweh is Salvation' and
though it was not an uncommon name in that day the name
here proclaimed the very message of the one who bore it. He
who was the Messiah, the 'Anointed One' or 'the Christ'
had come to express by word and work that 'Yahweh is
Salvation'.

Francis MacNutt, *The Healing Ministry*

I praise you, Father, for all that you are – your greatness is
beyond human comprehension. I worship you, because you

are worthy of praise. I bring my thanksgiving to you – for your goodness and love and especially for Jesus who is my Saviour.

*

You, O God, are my fortress, my loving God. Psalm 59:9

I am the vine; you are the branches. If a man remains in me and I in him, he will bear much fruit; apart from me you can do nothing. John 15:5

It is true that Saint Ignatius said, 'Act as though everything depended upon you'. But he added, 'But pray as though everything depended upon God'. God is the creator of the physical cosmos. He rules the stars as he rules the Church. And if, in his love, he has wished to make men his collaborators in the work of salvation, the limit of their power is very small and clearly defined. It is the limit of the wire compared with the electric current.

We are the wire, God is the current. Our only power is to let the current pass through us. Of course, we have the power to interrupt it and say 'No'. But nothing more.

Not, then, the image of the column acting as a support, but that of the wire allowing the current to pass through it. But the wire is one thing, the current is another. They are quite different, and there is certainly no reason for the wire to become self-satisfied, even one which transmits at high tension.

Carlo Carretto, *Letters From the Desert*

Teach me the truth of abiding, show me your purpose, which is that I should be truly usable by you.

*

To do your will, O my God, is my desire. Psalm 40:8

The foundation of the temple of the Lord was laid in the fourth year, in the month of Ziv. In the eleventh year in the month of Bul, the eighth month, the temple was finished in all its details according to its specifications. He had spent seven years building it. 1 Kings 6:37–38

It does not require much thought or time to draw the plan for a simple building, such as a chicken coop, barn or common dwelling, but it requires a long time to conceive the plan and draw the blueprint for a skyscraper, a cathedral or some other magnificent architectural structure. Because God's plans and plots for your life and mine are so magnificent, so far-reaching and so involved, it requires time for them to mature. The suspense and mystery connected with those plots and plans must be endured for a longer time, if anything great is to be accomplished through us. To change the picture, a mushroom comes up over night, but it requires a hundred years for an oak to mature.

Paul E. Billheimer, *The Mystery of His Providence*

Thank you for your patience, help me with my impatience, Father. Remind me that you are always in complete control;

although I long to be perfect I realize you are content to take all the time that is needed.

*

Holy, holy, holy is the Lord God Almighty, who was, and is, and is to come. Revelation 4:8

He shielded him and cared for him; he guarded him as the apple of his eye, like an eagle that stirs up its nest and hovers over its young, that spreads its wings to catch them and carries them on its pinions. The Lord alone led him; no foreign god was with him. Deuteronomy 32:10–12

We fail to understand the abiding love and care that God has for us. Not a love that smothers and seeks only to protect but a love that looks to make us strong. The eagle stirs the nest so that its young have to leave shelter and protection and take to the sky. That way the young birds use their wings and learn to fly. But just as the outstretched wings of the eagle are there underneath to catch and carry if there is need, so our God encourages us; we know that we must learn to be strong, but also that he will never leave us alone, he is always nearby to support us when the need arises.

Help me, Lord, as daily I try to please you in what I do. May I be strong and not fearful, remembering that you are always alongside.

Through the Morning
Available to God

Let us continually offer to God a sacrifice of praise. Hebrews 13:15

I am the good shepherd; I know my sheep and my sheep know me – just as the Father knows me and I know the Father – and I lay down my life for the sheep. John 10:14–15

Jesus is the Good Shepherd. He came in strength and courage to lead men back to God. Unceasingly he watches over his people, with them, as he promised, even to the end of the world. With gentle kindness he heals their diseases and comforts their sorrows and finds for them the food which is the living bread. With unwearied patience he bears with all their follies, their mistakes and their sins. And in the end he surrendered his life that they might be safe.

William Barclay, *Jesus As They Saw Him*

The love of Jesus is so deep and wonderful that sometimes I cannot truly understand it, Lord. Enable me to rest in it, help me to allow him to minister to me. Cause me to be quiet that I may feel his touch, and may my heart respond to his love.

*

Not to us, O Lord, not to us but to your name be the glory, because of your love and faithfulness. Psalm 115:1

Ask and it will be given to you; seek and you will find; knock and the door will be opened to you. For everyone who asks receives; he who seeks finds; and to him who knocks, the door will be opened. Matthew 7:7–8

Prayer consists of two parts, has two sides, a human and a divine. The human is the asking, the divine is the giving. Or, to look at both from the human side, there is the asking and the receiving – the two halves that make up a whole. It is as if he would tell us that we are not to rest without an answer, because it is the will of God, the rule in the Father's family; every childlike believing petition is granted. If no answer comes, we are not to sit down in the sloth that calls itself resignation and suppose that it is not God's will to give an answer. No; there must be something in the prayer that is not as God would have it, childlike and believing; we must seek for grace to pray so that the answer may come.

Andrew Murray, *With Christ in the School of Prayer*

I want to take hold of your promises; give me understanding, Lord, that I may become a strong believer enabling you to fulfil your word through me.

*

O Lord, what is man that you care for him, the son of man that you think of him? Psalm 144:3

Therefore, I urge you, brothers, in view of God's mercy, to offer your bodies as living sacrifices, holy and pleasing to God – which is your spiritual worship. Romans 12:1

God gives us his gift of faith to be Christian witnesses, his ambassadors. Not just to give and to go and to pray but to be. We are to be available to God. All the time, so that we can act in obedience (giving what he commands us); so that we can challenge the powers of darkness (going where he sends us); and so that we can keep on believing in the midst of every type of discouragement (praying as he burdens us). In all of this our faith will be tried, as gold by fire, purifying, refining, enriching it as we translate faith into service for him.

By faith we give ourselves wholly back to God to be available for the outworking of his perfect will. It is the presence of faith in our hearts that makes us want to give ourselves back to him. As by faith we appropriate God's gift of pardoning grace, and of power to be his witnesses, so we can make our response in obedience to his command to go and tell all nations. As we become involved with the Lord in this ministry of 'feeding the multitudes' we shall begin to understand something of the burden of God's heart for the needs of a lost world, and so pray that he will fill our hearts with his compassion for them.

Helen Roseveare, *Living Faith*

All that I need for all that you want of me can be found in you. Increase my faith that I may be strong for any task that you have for me to do.

*

I will praise the Lord. Psalm 16:7

A new commandment I give you: Love one another. As I have loved you, so you must love one another. All men will know that you are my disciples if you love one another. John 13: 34–35

Thanking, adoring and contemplating are the primary acts in the Christian use of praying, because in the Christian understanding of experience there is so much to praise and love, and because the more the self is turned to the non-self in communion the more it becomes itself as created by God instead of the self-made distortion of this we carry around most of the time. The more the real self is freed from what we think it is or feel it ought to be and is allowed to be the alive centre of our existence, the more we can treat other people with a similar relaxation and generosity. We stop wanting them to measure up to our requirements, we are able to accept them as they are, we find that there is room in our thoughts for other beings, as alive and awkward and needy as ourselves. This is to walk out of the self into the real world, the only world in which genuine love is possible.

J. Neville Ward, *The Use of Praying*

Give me the desire to spend time with you, Lord, that looking at you I may forget myself and draw from you what I need to love others with your love.

*

May my meditation be pleasing to him, as I rejoice in the Lord. Psalm 104:34

Our fathers disciplined us for a little while as they thought best; but God disciplines us for our good, that we may share in his holiness. Hebrews 12:10

God's chastening is not punishment for its own sake but always to correct. It always has a definite aim; to correct, to equip, to prepare for something round the corner. God's chastening is preparation. In a word: chastening always has a redemptive purpose. It is never carried out by God to 'get even' with us. God 'got even' at the cross. Chastening ought not to be regarded as God's way of satisfying himself. Parents do this, yes, we parents chasten our own with partly selfish motives. Holiness, that is the purpose of God in chastening us. None of us takes to holiness naturally. We are all congenitally allergic to holiness. It is easier to watch television than to pray, easier to read a magazine than to read the Bible. All of us have a tendency to impute more spirituality to ourselves than is there. Chastening is so often the only way by which we see ourselves with true objectivity. God is the only infallible parent. He never loses his temper. When he metes out chastening it is carefully designed, carefully planned, carefully thought out. For God chastens for one reason only; for our good. It is not for himself but for our profit.

R. T. Kendall, *Once Saved, Always Saved*

Help me, Father, to understand that the chastening that comes into my life comes from your love. Enable me to learn your lessons quickly.

*

I will praise your name, O Lord, for it is good. Psalm 54:6

For in the gospel a righteousness from God is revealed, a righteousness that is by faith from first to last, just as it is written: 'The righteous will live by faith.' Romans 1:17

If we only believe, there is no limit to the blessings God will give us. We are told that Christ came to give us an abundant life. That means something far beyond the narrow, limited, frustrated lives most of us live. The whole emphasis of the New Testament which we so tragically miss is that God wants to pour out blessings in overflowing generosity. No blessing is too great, no power too strong, no victory too complete. All is ours. We read a strange statement in the New Testament; Christ had been depicting the wonders God wants to give to people and was telling them what they could have and do and be. But he saw that they did not believe him, would not accept what was offered, and we read that 'he marvelled because of their unbelief'. He was bewildered because people who were offered everything chose to continue living on nothing. So today the average man lives on spiritual relief when all of God's riches are his for the taking.

Norman Vincent Peale and Smiley Blanton,
Faith is the Answer

You said, Lord, that we only need faith as a grain of mustard seed. Enlarge my faith that I may not disappoint you by not being able to enter into the riches that you have for me.

*

Great are the works of the Lord. Psalm 111:2

Then you will call upon me and come and pray to me, and I will listen to you. You will seek me and find me when you seek me with all your heart. Jeremiah 29:12–13

He makes a direct call to us for single-mindedness, a single-minded longing for him – no lesser aim will do; no desire to be good; no striving to measure up to some standard we have set for ourselves, to correct some failure we have been shown in our way of life. These may be temporarily necessary but they will turn to dust and ashes – they will end in a grim dryness – unless at the back of them all is what he asks of us – a never-ending search for a real knowledge of him, for a sense of his reality, a confidence in his companionship, a joy and delight in the very person of God himself. It is for this that we must learn to long and long, till our prayers for it become not just a form of words, but a stretching out of our whole being to him.

Florence Allshorn, *The Notebooks of Florence Allshorn*

Thank you for the comfort of your word. Cause me to persevere in my searching for you, that I may know you more and more.

*

It is I who made the earth and created mankind upon it. Isaiah 45:12

Come, let us bow down in worship, let us kneel before the Lord our Maker; for he is our God and we are the people of his pasture, the flock under his care. Psalm 95:6–7

In this age, when mystery and transcendence are suspect, there still remains in the human make-up a profound need to worship. Granted the need, it would be mere contrivance to fix on Christ for the purpose of fulfilling that need. We must look at it the other way round, and call, if not on our own experience, on the observed experience of countless witnesses. It was from a context of doubt that the restored relationship of person to Person at once intensified into the words of worship 'My Lord and my God'; and since the first recorded Easter meetings, the centuries have been spanned by a great host of witnesses, of those who have lived and died and lived again in a knowledge to which worship is always the first spontaneous reaction. It is not that the instinct to worship has at last contrived a focus but that the relationship once entered can be expressed in nothing else. We have no power of ourselves – or, it seems, not quite enough power – to help ourselves, not even to belief. Belief remains a gift. We have perhaps just enough power to pray that God will fetch us to belief, or that he will fortify the belief we already hold.

Robert Runcie, *Windows Onto God*

Thank you for the gift of your Holy Spirit and for his working in my life. May I always be open to him, so that through his power I may give you the worship due to your name.

*

The Lord lives! Praise be to my Rock! Psalm 18:46

So then, men ought to regard us as servants of Christ and as those entrusted with the secret things of God. Now it is required that those who have been given a trust must prove faithful. 1 Corinthians 4:1–2

God must rejoice when he sees his servants following his will, enduring hardship and pain for the sake of the Gospel. How often we marvel at the saints who have done such great things for God. It is not all in the past either; in our day we see those who faithfully preach, travel and minister for God. We know the names of many who seem to have such committed and fruitful lives. It is difficult to remember when we are trying to keep a family together, coping with the myriad of things that have to be done in a home, that we can be as much in God's plan as any of those we mistakenly feel are doing more for him. Being faithful can just as much be nurturing children at home as going thousands of miles away to minister to those who do not know of Christ. Perhaps we feel there is a difference because ministers and missionaries are in situations in which they know that they cannot manage on their own. They have to spend time with God and depend on the Holy Spirit for the work they do, so much of which they know that they cannot do of themselves. Whoever heard of not being able to cope with the washing up? But we also need the Holy Spirit's help in our attitude to the unwashed dishes. Depending on him could mean a better organized day, less frustration, a happier atmosphere for those around us.

If it is God's plan for a woman to be a mother and to run a home, then he surely intends her to depend on him as much as do any other of his children. We may call some tasks mundane and routine, but I doubt that he does.

Thank you for reminding me that you have planned my life, and that as I have tried to follow you, so this is where I should be. I want my attitude to be right to all that has to be done, so that you may be glorified and may find pleasure in me.

*

You who fear the Lord, praise him! Psalm 22:23

Blessed are they whose ways are blameless, who walk according to the law of the Lord. Blessed are they who keep his statutes and seek him with all their heart. Psalm 119:1–2

There is a widespread impression that the gift of contemplation is an abnormal phenomenon in human life, restricted to a few especially chosen souls, most of whom withdraw completely from everyday life. But while this gift of contemplation in its fullness is the crown of spiritual life and the direct gift of God alone, it should in some sense be the goal of all who seek God, and it is granted to a greater or lesser degree to all who earnestly seek to love God with all their heart, mind, soul and strength, this degree depending upon the soul's progress in the life of prayer. Prayer is mankind's highest activity, and like all other activities develops from small beginnings and reaches its goal in many varied ways. The intensity of the love of one human being for another is dependent upon the degree to which the loved one occupies the heart and mind of the lover; similarly, the intensity of man's love and the depth of his experience of

God depends upon the degree to which God occupies the heart and mind of one who seeks him. When a man devotes himself to know and love God with his whole heart, mind, soul and strength, God grants his gift of love and contemplation through and in which lover and Beloved are united.

Leo Sherley Price,
Introduction, *The Ladder of Perfection*

Your face would I seek, O Lord, your heart would I know.

*

I am the first and I am the last; apart from me there is no God. Isaiah 44:6

And we, who with unveiled faces all reflect the Lord's glory, are being transformed into his likeness with ever-increasing glory, which comes from the Lord, who is the Spirit. 2 Corinthians 3:18

Conversion brings other benefits besides forgiveness. God promises that those who turn to him will be inwardly changed. They will be 'born anew' into a new kind of life, with new aims and perspectives – with new hopes, new inner resources and a new Jesus life style. The source of this quiet revolution is God's Spirit. He moves in with us as soon as we respond to his inward persuasion to turn to Christ. And he lives out in us the powerful new life that Jesus released into the world by defeating sin and death. The Holy Spirit brings us into the whole new world and, as we learn to co-operate with him and rely on his power, we begin to be transformed into Jesus' likeness. Because we still belong to a rebel race and because sin has done us permanent damage, we will never (in this life) be perfect or completely Christ-like. But inwardly we have begun to be like him. Day by day we can become more and more Christ-like outwardly until finally, in heaven, we shall resemble him perfectly.

> David Hewetson and David Miller,
> *Christianity Made Simple*

Thank you, Father, for the gift of your Spirit and the work that he does in our lives of transforming us and making us more like Jesus.

*

May the peoples praise you, O God; may all the peoples praise you. Psalm 67:5

Blessed is the man who does not walk in the counsel of the wicked or stand in the way of sinners or sit in the seat of mockers. But his delight is in the law of the Lord, and on his law he meditates day and night. Psalm 1:1–2

When the heart has received the Word through the mind, and has had its spiritual powers called out and exercised on it, the Word is no longer void, but has done that whereunto God has sent it. It has become part of our life, and strengthened us for new purpose and effort. It is in meditation that the heart holds and appropriates the Word. Just as in reflection the understanding grasps all the meaning and bearings of a truth, so in meditation the heart assimilates it and makes it a part of its own life. We need continual reminding that the heart means the will and the affection. The meditation of the heart implies desire, acceptance, surrender, love. Out of the heart are the issues of life; what the heart truly believes, that it receives with love and joy, and allows to master and rule the life. The intellect gathers and prepares the food on which we are to feed. In meditation the heart takes it in and feeds on it.

Andrew Murray, The Best of Andrew Murray

Cause my heart to desire you and to meditate on your ways, O Lord.

*

Surely God is my salvation. Isaiah 12:2

Then Jesus said to his disciples, 'If anyone would come after me, he must deny himself and take up his cross and follow me.' Matthew 16:24

There is a danger of constructing a spirituality which will not face up to the Cross as a predominant element. Some spiritual writers today seem to forget that our Lord said 'let him take up his cross and follow me'. We shrink from the Cross because it is the natural, almost the right, thing to do. Like the apostles, we are overcome with fear. It is right that we should work to rid ourselves of those things which we call the 'Cross', whether personal problems or day to day practical difficulties. But we need to remind ourselves again and again that the Cross is and must be an element in a life in which we truly follow Christ.

Basil Hume, OSB, *Searching for God*

You set your face towards the Cross, Lord, and you suffered it for me. Show me what your words should mean for me in my Christian life.

*

You are the God who performs miracles. Psalm 77:14

Surely he took up our infirmities and carried our sorrows, yet we considered him stricken by God, smitten by him, and afflicted. But he was pierced for our transgressions, he was crushed for our iniquities; the punishment that brought us peace was upon him, and by his wounds we are healed. Isaiah 53:4–5

I cannot tell why He, whom angels worship,
    Should set His love upon the sons of men,
Or why, as Shepherd, He should seek the wanderers,
    To bring them back, they know not how or when.
But this I know, that He was born of Mary,
    When Bethlehem's manger was His only home,
And that He lived at Nazareth and laboured,
    And so the Saviour, Saviour of the world, is come.

I cannot tell how silently He suffered,
　As with His peace He graced this place of tears,
Or how His heart upon the Cross was broken,
　The crown of pain to three and thirty years.
But this I know, He heals the broken hearted,
　And stays our sin, and calms our lurking fear,
And lifts the burden from the heavy laden,
　For yet the Saviour, Saviour of the world, is here.

William Young Fullerton

We can never know fully, Lord, just what it cost you to live and die on this earth. Only as I draw nearer to you shall I perhaps understand a little more. Help me not to be complacent or to take all the benefits of your life and death for granted, but to seek humbly to enter into the fellowship of your suffering.

*

Praise be to the Lord, the God of Israel, because he has come and has redeemed his people. Luke 1:68

Make every effort to live in peace with all men and to be holy; without holiness no one will see the Lord. Hebrews 12:14

It is very important for the comprehension of holiness to understand that it has two poles: *God* and the *World*. Its source, its fulcrum and its content is God, but its point of impact, the place into which it is born, where it develops and also where it is expressed in terms of Christ's salvation, is the world, this ambiguous world which, on the one hand, was created by God and is the object of such love that the Father gave his only-begotten Son for its salvation, and on the other hand, has fallen into the slavery of evil. This pole of holiness which relates to the world therefore has two aspects: a vision of the world as God willed it, as he loves it, and at the same time an asceticism which requires us to disengage ourselves from the world and free the world from the grip of Satan. This second element, this battle which is our vocation, is part and parcel of holiness.

Anthony Bloom, *God and Man*

Father, help me to remember that it is the world that you love and for whom your Son died. Make me usable in the task of revealing the good news of salvation.

*

Sing to God . . . sing praise to the Lord. Psalm 68:32

The fruit of the Spirit is love, joy, peace, patience, kindness, goodness, faithfulness, gentleness and self-control. Galatians 5:22–23

Although these fruits are deep interior qualities enriching the receiver, yet they are not inward looking. They originate in God's action within us to create a new relationship with our fellow men. Do not love, joy, peace, patience, kindness, generosity, self-control manifestly create a new and God-given relationship to our neighbour? And one that is devoid of the pretence which is so common a feature of our ordinary social relationships? It is devoid of all pretence because it proceeds from qualities that are transparently real, true love for our neighbour, true joy in our heart creating a feeling of desiring to give what has been so freely given to us, true peace because the egoistic motives for battle have vanished, true patience and not mere toleration, and a steady kindness, for are we not conscious of receiving the kindness of our God every moment of our lives?

Faithfulness here is that quality or fruit that really believes and trusts God, and accepts his will and praises him, when the circumstances of life might prompt a very different reaction. It is the quality that, by absolute trust, overcomes and knows that God on his side is ever faithful and full of loving kindness.

David Parry, *This Promise is for You*

I pray, Lord, that the harvest of these fruits of the Spirit may be great in my life. The more that these are seen, the more you are seen and I truly want to diminish in order that you may be magnified.

*

The Lord watches over the way of the righteous. Psalm 1:6

As God has said: 'I will live with them and walk among them, and I will be their God, and they will be my people.' 2 Corinthians 6:16

The greatest need we have – as individuals, as communities, as a world – is to 'get it all together'. We need 'wholeness'. We need 'health'. The Bible's word for it is 'holiness'. We are quite wrong to think of a holy man as someone with a prayer book in one hand, a halo in the other and a benign smile on his face. Holiness is far more exciting than that. A holy person is a whole person – a person who is right with God, and who really makes the most of life, both for himself and others. Holiness is never the result of self-improvement. It comes from knowing God.

Andrew Knowles, *Finding Faith*

May I be a whole person, Lord. Touch and heal in every part, so that my mind, body and spirit glorify you.

Noontime
Going On With the Lord

I will sing to the Lord, for he is highly exalted. Exodus 15:1

Be self-controlled and alert. Your enemy the devil prowls around like a roaring lion looking for someone to devour. Resist him, standing firm in the faith, because you know that your brothers throughout the world are undergoing the same kind of sufferings. 1 Peter 5:8–9

The Church at large seems to have lost the recognition that there is a war on. 'Church' is a place to go on a Sunday once a week – or once a month – not a corps of battle troops under a Commander against a skilful, powerful, ruthless foe. Camouflage is one of the basic arts of warfare. If the enemy has managed to camouflage himself so well that most churchmen do not notice he is around or even believe he exists – well that suits him admirably. Such a church is easy prey for him. But the early Christians were under no illusions. They believed in a devil who was like a roaring lion, like an angel in disguise, like an experienced wrestler, like the best soldiery known to antiquity.

Michael Green, *I Believe in Satan's Downfall*

Lord, keep me aware of the spiritual warfare that is continually being waged. May my life be so hid in Christ that I stand fast at all times against the assaults of the enemy.

*

Noontime

My soul praises the Lord and my spirit rejoices in God my
Saviour. Luke 1:46–47

Love is patient, love is kind. It does not envy, it does not
boast, it is not proud. It is not rude, it is not self-seeking,
it is not easily angered, it keeps no records of wrongs.
1 Corinthians 13:4–5

What did St Paul mean in his great hymn to love when he
said that 'love does not keep a record of wrongs' (GNB)? –
he meant that to love we must be able to believe that
people's characters do alter, that the leopard *can* change its
spots, that conversions do occur, that people do repent and
that at times they do change. To put it another way, he
was urging that when we are in relationships of long
standing we must live in the present, not in the past. For
sooner or later, in any friendship, someone will be
wronged. In a weak moment, the beloved will desert us or
severely criticize us or embarrass us, or walk away from
us. And if we allow ourselves to dwell on these misdeeds,
the relationship is doomed. Keeping closed books on how
many wrongs have been done us makes us become accusa-
tory, for most of us have a short memory for our own
mistakes.

If we are to forgive freely, we need a tolerance of others
as generous as that tolerance we display toward our own
errors.

Alan Loy McGinnis, *The Friendship Factor*

Please help me to remember that my friends work at their
spiritual life in the same way that I do. Instead of being
upset by what I might consider less than perfect behaviour, grant me a greater understanding and love. Enable
me to forgive when that is needed. At all times keep me

43

remembering that I have the same failures as I tend to see in others.

*

The Lord reigns, let the earth be glad. Psalm 97:1

Remember this: Whoever sows sparingly will also reap sparingly, and whoever sows generously will also reap generously. Each man should give what he has decided in his heart to give, not reluctantly or under compulsion, for God loves a cheerful giver. 2 Corinthians 9:6–7

Decane Logsden, an American millionaire, once said that the greatest test in his life had been that of affluence, even though he and his family had also been very poor and had gone through other times of great testing. With sufficiency of money we tend to turn away from God because we feel that we are able to meet our own needs. Then the amount that we think about giving to God's work, even just ten per cent of our incomes, seems large and we may be tempted to want to keep more back for ourselves, forgetting that he gave it to us in the first place. The things that money can buy seem good until we begin to realize the growing poverty of our spirit. We then need renewed thinking so that we understand that whatever we have has been given to us as stewards, to be used for God's work and the advancement of his Kingdom.

Lord, help me to see that the things I have are really yours. Teach me how to share or give to your people with real joy.

*

O Lord, open my lips, and my mouth will declare your praise. Psalm 51:15

And let us consider how we may spur one another on towards love and good deeds. Let us not give up meeting together, as some are in the habit of doing, but let us encourage one another – and all the more as you see the Day approaching. Hebrews 10:24–25

When you stop to analyse the concept, 'encourage' takes on a new meaning. It's the act of inspiring others with renewed courage, spirit or hope. When we encourage others we spur them on, we stimulate and affirm them. It is helpful to remember the distinction between appreciation and affirmation. We appreciate what a person does, but we affirm who a person is. Appreciation comes and goes because it is usually related to something someone accomplishes. Affirmation goes deeper. It is directed to the person himself or herself.

Charles R. Swindoll, *Strengthening Your Grip*

Help me to think the best of people, Lord, to the extent that I forget myself and am concerned with others and their feelings. May I encourage others by a right attitude and the right words.

*

My help comes from the Lord, the Maker of heaven and earth. Psalm 121:2

My heart is not proud, O Lord, my eyes are not haughty; I do not concern myself with great matters or things too wonderful for me. But I have stilled and quieted my soul; like a weaned child with its mother, like a weaned child is my soul within me. Psalm 131:1–2

For years I had tried desperately to belong, to be accepted by the world around me – whether it was the world of Hitler's youth marching in the neighbourhood park or the world of a pastor's wife fitting into a preconceived mould of perfection.

Now I felt acceptable to myself, I thanked God for allowing me all the experiences of my past – even my inability to bear children. I realized that I had a part to play in the Lord's plan and had been called to a special service. Why should I be afraid to face my strengths and weaknesses, my fears and failures, my talents and goals any longer? My goal, I knew without question, was to grow to be more like Jesus – not a chameleon whose colours change depending on its environment.

If God accepted me with all my failures and shortcomings, my cracks and creaks, my nicks and bruises, wasn't it about time I accepted myself?

Jutta Jarnagin, *The Raging*

O Father, do not let my heart be proud – do not allow me to try to do things beyond my strength and your will. Help me not only to accept myself as I am, but also all my circumstances just as they are, so that in acceptance I may glorify you.

*

Be exalted, O God, above the heavens, and let your glory be over all the earth. Psalm 108:5

So God created man in his own image, in the image of God he created him; male and female he created them. Genesis 1:27

Sexuality is knowing ourselves deeply as a man or a woman; it is realizing that men and women are different and have different emotional responses in the same situation. Discovering one's sexuality means finding out that to be a woman is satisfactory and not second class; that it is acceptable to be not quite so tough, and sometimes slightly more intuitive than logical. It means realizing that getting out of the woman box of feeble femininity does not force one into an aggressive women's liberation box.

Faith Lees, *Break Open My World*

Thank you for making me. Help me to come to terms with what I am and enable me to walk daily rejoicing in your plan for my life.

*

The Lord is compassionate and gracious. Psalm 103:8

Defend the cause of the weak and fatherless; maintain the rights of the poor and oppressed. Rescue the weak and needy; deliver them from the hand of the wicked. Psalm 82:3–4

So often we defend our own way of life, rather than take up the cause of those in need. Our view of the poor or the unemployed can be that if they are in these categories somehow it is their own fault: the poor mismanage the money they have or spend it on foolish things, we think; the unemployed should look harder for a job or be willing to do any sort of work. Our thoughts about them take on a superiority that ill behoves us if we have never sat where they sit. Our Lord expects those who follow him to look after those in need – *all* who are in need, not just those to whom it is easy to give, but also the down-and-out who offend us in sight and smell. Not just a Society who works amongst those in our own country but in countries in other parts of the world. And if money is easy to give perhaps we should be giving something else – actively taking part in a cause that affects the lives of other human beings, just helping someone to obtain her rights, or giving more practical help and advice.

We glibly say that Jesus has no hands but our hands; how sad it is that so many are idle when there is so much to be done.

Forgive me for my wrong attitudes and my lack of giving when confronted by the needs of others. Teach me to have a greater understanding of those in less fortunate situations than myself; teach me to be willing to share in whatever way you prompt me.

*

The Lord is gracious and compassionate. Psalm 145:8

Pray also for me, that whenever I open my mouth, words may be given me so that I will fearlessly make known the mystery of the gospel, for which I am an ambassador in chains. Pray that I may declare it fearlessly, as I should. Ephesians 6:19–20

It's so easy for us to live in a Christian cocoon. We spend Sunday with believers, we meet believers in the week, we have friends who are believers, and we go out with them, we go on holidays with believers, and so on. Personally, I like being with believers, and if it were left to me, I would spend all my time with them, but that would leave the non-believing world without any bridges. If bridges were taken out of the physical world, we'd all be in trouble. Yet in the spiritual sense many of us seem quite content to let the non-believing world get by without them.

Jim Smith, *Time to Share*

Father, put your desires in my heart, that I may be used to help others to know you.

*

This is the Lord . . . let us rejoice and be glad in his salvation. Isaiah 25:9

'Love the Lord your God with all your heart and with all your soul and with all your strength and with all your mind', and 'Love your neighbour as yourself'. Luke 10:27

Justice and love are the two absolute moral commandments. They cover every conceivable human situation. There is no nook or cranny in our lives together in which we may ignore the demands of justice and love. Everything we do must be fair; if it is not fair, it is not right. And everything we do must be helpful, or at least not hurtful: if we mean it to hurt and not help people, it is not right. Justice holds us back in respect, it tells us to let people be what they are and have what they have. Love pushes us toward people in care; it tells us to get into people's lives so that we can help them be what they ought to be and get what they ought to have. Justice and love are the absolutes of life to which the other commandments point. The other commands are valid because they direct us to embody justice and love in the complex realities of human life.

Lewis Smedes, *Mere Morality*

Only in your strength is it possible to love others and to serve others faithfully. Keep me open to you, Lord, that you may show yourself through me.

*

Sing to the Lord, you saints of his; praise his holy name. Psalm 30:4

So do not fear, for I am with you; do not be dismayed, for I am your God. I will strengthen you and help you; I will uphold you with my righteous right hand. Isaiah 41:10

It is in our nature to fear the unknown, whether it be the events of tomorrow or the thought of something greater. How would I manage under persecution? how shall I cope with old age? we wonder, and our heart fails within us. Yet testimony points to the fact that in the moments of crisis, if we but turn our face towards God, stretch out a hand however weakly to him, murmur but a single word of appeal, he will respond. The wonderful thing is that he is so eager to share in our lives. Nothing is too trivial to claim his attention. It is not the circumstances, but the person going through them that matters to him. So day by day, as the smaller things are committed to him, I shall in a sense be in practice for the bigger things. As we habitually hand over the details of our lives, so we shall have learnt dependence for whatever comes.

Forgive me that so often I am fearful, that I forget your promises to be with me. Strengthen my faith that I may prove you, that I may do the things you want of me in calmness and peace, secure in the knowledge of your love.

*

'Do I not fill heaven and earth?' declares the Lord. Jeremiah 23:24

For I am convinced that neither death nor life, neither angels nor demons, neither the present nor the future, nor any powers, neither height nor depth, nor anything else in all creation, will be able to separate us from the love of God that is in Christ Jesus our Lord. Romans 8:38–39

Can you believe this? Will you believe this? If you will, God can change your life. You will be able to live confidently no matter what tests may come your way, no matter what happens. Nothing can change God's love for you. That's worth thinking about when danger, trouble, accident or death strike. Sometimes Christians feel that they should be delivered from accidents, sickness and death. And when trouble comes they ask: 'Why did God let this happen to me?' The Bible does not promise escape from suffering. If it did, then everybody would become a Christian just to avoid accidents, troubles, heart attacks, cancer. That might be a good motive for being religious, but it's a poor motive for being a Christian. Instead God offers us his presence in all of life's troubles. He tells us that nothing can ever shake his love for us. For the Christian every cloud doesn't have a silver lining, but *behind the clouds the sun is always shining*.

Fritz Ridenour,
How to be a Christian without being Religious

In you is everything that I need. Keep my eyes fixed on you, Lord, that I may ever walk with you in confidence and trust.

*

You are my Lord; apart from you I have no good thing. Psalm 16:2

As the time approached for him to be taken up to heaven, Jesus resolutely set out for Jerusalem. Luke 9:51

When Jesus came on this earth he was born in a stable, he lived the life of a village boy, eventually taking up a trade. He must have gone through all the normal ups and downs of family life, anxieties, new life, death. At a certain time he began the ministry that meant leaving his home and going out as an itinerant preacher. His message was a radical one, the authorities took notice of him, life began to be less normal and less easy. There were times when he was tired and weary, when the task he had set out to do must have seemed very heavy. Could he have been lonely? Even despondent? Yet he was firmly set on his course. Jesus knew that above everything he was to be obedient to his heavenly Father, was faithfully to follow his will. And as we know he did, he followed obediently right through to death.

If we try to live our life in the light of his, then we should be able to learn to set aside our self-pity and follow the way that is set before us, just as he did. Only we must never try to do it alone. We have resources to draw on, and if we do not do so, we must never say that God has in any way failed us. We fail him when we neglect or refuse to live spiritually with him. That is when things go wrong. Like Jesus we should go through the days of life, in the place and sphere in which God has placed us, determined to fulfil the plan God has for us.

I want my eyes to be fixed on you, Lord; I want to go forward in the life and way that you have set me as resolutely as I can, depending on you for all my strength and courage.

*

For you, O Lord, have delivered my soul from death. Psalm 116:8

Your attitude should be the same as that of Christ Jesus: who, being in very nature God, did not consider equality with God something to be grasped, but made himself nothing, taking the very nature of a servant, being made in human likeness. Philippians 2:6–7

Some of us go through life expecting other people to make it easy for us. We think that we deserve love and help – encouragement when we fall down, sensitivity to our moods. We want people to be interested in us, turn aside and speak to us, notice us at all times. If we do not get this attention then it is 'they' who are peculiar, unfeeling, disinterested, lacking in love. The sooner we disabuse ourselves concerning the place that we think we should hold in the esteem of others, the sooner we shall understand what it means to walk with God. When we can take the words of the prayer of St Francis and really try to do what they say then we shall have something more of the life of Christ within us. By seeking to console rather than be consoled, to understand than to be understood, to love rather than to be loved, we shall forget self and find more happiness than if we only brood on ourselves.

Christ washed the feet of his disciples, something that astonished them: how far are we willing to go in giving of ourselves to others?

May my attitude be that of love and caring, seeking to forget myself and thinking always of others first.

*

Give thanks to the Lord, call on his name; make known among the nations what he has done. Psalm 105:1

I urge, then, first of all, that requests, prayers, intercession and thanksgiving be made for everyone – for kings and all those in authority, that we may live peaceful and quiet lives in all godliness and holiness. This is good, and pleases God our Saviour, who wants all men to be saved and to come to a knowledge of the truth. 1 Timothy 2:1–4

Prayer for leaders requires a world vision, a sense of history and an attention to detail. World vision comes by keeping ourselves informed and by deliberately avoiding mere parochialism in our prayer concern. A sense of history will stop us from expecting too much too quickly, as well as being alert to the suddenness with which events can happen on the world scene. We will try to perceive the long-term purpose of God. An attention to detail will avoid our being vague. Information on the countries of the world and their leaders is available, enabling us to pray by name for rulers and to have some understanding of the political structure of a country. Similarly, in praying for people who wield enormous influence in commerce, trade unions or politics, it is good to pray with names.

What do we pray about? Certainly not for their well-being or success. We pray for leaders because of their effect on countries but the movement of 1 Timothy 2:1–3 leads us on to the spreading of the Gospel as the supreme objective of our praying.

Michael Baughen, *The Prayer Principle*

Guide the leaders of the nations into the ways of peace and

justice and lead them into a knowledge of Jesus Christ. May those who are Christians be strong in seeking to know and carry out your will, that peoples everywhere may want to follow you.

Time for Those Near to Me
Bind Us Together

Let the name of the Lord be praised, both now and for evermore. Psalm 113:2

Every year his parents went to Jerusalem for the Feast of the Passover. When he was twelve years old, they went up to the Feast, according to the custom. After the Feast was over, while his parents were returning home, the boy Jesus stayed behind in Jerusalem, but they were unaware of it. Luke 2:41–43

So Jesus's parents lose him when he is twelve years old, and three days later find a son who has gone through the biblical 'three days', has died and risen into a new dimension and now speaks about a mysterious concern with God that has taken him from them. He has begun his own journey into the interior of life.

Everything in life exists for this solitary journey of each individual toward his own grasp of life's meaning and his freedom to love. Marriage itself is for this, to lead husband and wife to their individual experience of life's meaning and then joy in the fullest and most varied loving possible to them. God has willed that they make much of this journey together, find freedom of love to some extent through each other, each the minister of the grace of their sacrament to the other, but marriage is not the goal of their life. Loving is the goal, which means that God is the goal who is himself love and can alone free our loving from all that inhibits it. This love which is God is infinite love, and the more a husband and wife have of it the more of life they will be able to love. It will enrich what is between them but it will also take them from each other. Because their individual loving has fulfilled each as a self and they have not confined their loving to their marriage, each will have more to give the other.

J. Neville Ward, *Five for Sorrow, Ten for Joy*

Each person has to find you, Lord, for himself. As I learn to live with you each day, may it mean that my relationships with others will also have a greater dimension. Marriage, children, friends and even acquaintances should be touched by what I receive from you. May it be so.

*

Surely God is my help; the Lord is the one who sustains me. Psalm 54:4

With the tongue we praise our Lord and Father, and with it we curse men, who have been made in God's likeness. Out of the same mouth come praise and cursing. My brothers, this should not be. Can both fresh water and salt water flow from the same spring? James 3:9–11

How easy it is to be destructive in our thinking and speech, to pull down instead of build up, to deflate and criticize instead of encourage. Why is it that we must always see the faults in others, notice the weaknesses and failures, and fail to see the strengths? Situations also defeat us; much is wrong, little is right. We opt out so easily when things are not going the way that we feel they should be. We completely refuse to look from anyone else's viewpoint, we ride our hobby horse, never stopping to wonder whether our attitude is in any way inflicting hurt or pain. If instead of complaining to others we took everything to God constructively, praying and thinking about situations in the way that we feel he would prefer us to think about them, seeing people as he does, in all their potential, then things would change; they would change more quickly than if we just continued to grumble, for we should begin to see the good in others and be more concerned about them as people.

Keep me so close to you, Lord, that I think only of encouraging and helping others and not of complaining and criticizing.

*

Sing to him, sing praise to him; tell of all his wonderful acts.
Psalm 105:2

Then the Lord God made a woman from the rib he had taken out of the man and he brought her to the man.
Genesis 2:22

Woman must continually remind man in his pride that he is incomplete. She must remind man in his egoism that he must transcend himself. She must remind the world that it compromises its noblest aspirations when it makes light of the human person and that the spirit of man cannot bring the world to completion without the help of God. Modern man desperately needs woman, her insights, her tenderness, her graciousness, her sense of personal values, her concern for detail, her ability to adapt herself – so that our institutions, our laws, our way of life may be made responsive to the values of the person, and so that a world may come into being in which men can achieve their supernatural destiny. The promotion of woman will occur when she becomes fully aware of her responsibility in regard to the building of the world and when she is willing to be present in the world and to play her proper role in it at every time, economic, political, social, in short, from the small cell of the family to the complex organizations of society. Then will the world find completion, the world which at the beginning God entrusted to both man and woman.

Michel Quoist, *The Christian Response*

Father, when you created man and woman, you knew exactly what you were doing. You made us different in so many ways, but that was the plan. Help me to do what is natural and right for me as a woman, to carry out my role under your guidance in the way that glorifies you.

*

Praise the Lord. Praise the Lord, O my soul. Psalm 146:1

'For this reason a man will leave his father and mother and be united to his wife, and the two will become one flesh.'

This is a profound mystery – but I am talking about Christ and the church. However, each one of you also must love his wife as he loves himself, and the wife must respect her husband. Ephesians 5:31–33

What is a marriage encounter? It begins with a simple fact! There is often a lack of real communication between married couples, even in good solid marriages. Experience shows that over a period of years, married life can become a routine co-existence in which each spouse is preoccupied with a series of duties, which leave no time for a deep sharing of personal life in all its dimensions. If married love is to be genuine, it must be a communion of soul, spirit, heart and body. Communion of soul means that life is really shared in its depth, and that both partners are able to mutually communicate what is deepest within them.

Communion of spirit means deep oneness in the way they both look at life and its fundamental problems.

Communion of heart means mutual affection, gift of self, sharing in full the existence of the other.

Communion of the body means physical union as the bodily expression of the sentiments of the soul.

Léon Joseph, Cardinal Suenens, *A New Pentecost?*

Father, I ask for your working in and through the sacrament of marriage. Grant a new strengthening and commitment on the part of those who have been called by you into this contract. May your purposes be fully carried out for each partnership, and the deepening relationship to each other mean also a deeper relationship with you.

*

I am the Lord, your God. Isaiah 43:3

It is not for you to know the times or dates the Father has set by his own authority. But you will receive power when the Holy Spirit comes on you; and you will be my witnesses in Jerusalem, and in all Judea and Samaria, and to the ends of the earth. Acts 1:7–8

The Plan. 'You will be witnesses for me.'
The Scope. 'In Jerusalem, in all Judea and Samaria and to the ends of the earth.' (That is, in ever-widening circles, beginning nearest home.)
The Secret. 'When the Holy Spirit comes upon you, you will be filled with power.'

Every Christian lives in a world of natural contacts. We have family relatives, school friends, work mates, fellow commuters, fellow students, neighbours. Other Mums meet their children at the school gates, people bump into us playing squash, watching football, collecting train numbers, or jogging. We meet people at parent-teacher associations, ratepayers' protest meetings, trade union meetings. God has made these people our mission field. Few of us will be called to dramatic pioneer missionary work. Not many of us are ordained to the ministry. But each of us is to be a witness.

Donald Bridge and David Phypers,
Growing in God's Family

Take away my fears and by the power of your Spirit help me to speak for you. Give me the opportunities, and the courage to take them.

*

How great is your goodness. Psalm 31:19

Be completely humble and gentle; be patient, bearing with one another in love. Make every effort to keep the unity of the Spirit through the bond of peace. Ephesians 4:2–3

Into our marriage came an ever-deepening fusion of heart and mind, though never a static peace. It was a harmony growing out of diversity in unity, the most melodious harmony there is. . . . His job was constantly to pour himself out for the hungry hearts of men and women. My job was to try to feed him spiritually, to strengthen him, to supply understanding and encouragement, so that he would always have something to give to others.

We came to see this oneness between us as the open door by which the Spirit of God poured into our lives and work. When that agreement was missing, the door was closed, we were 'on our own'; our work was self-managed, fruitless. . . .

It was the same invaluable lesson that the Apostles had learned at Pentecost. Like those first disciples, we discovered that the results of real accord could be breathtaking, limitless.

Catherine Marshall, *A Man Called Peter*

The partnership that you give, Lord, can grow and deepen. May the door be always open for your Spirit so that our union is ever one of enrichment to us and glory to you.

*

'I am the Alpha and the Omega,' says the Lord God.
Revelation 1:8

We who are strong ought to bear with the failings of the
weak and not to please ourselves. Each of us should please
his neighbour for his good, to build him up. Romans 15:1–2

Marriage is not being chained to each other all the time, it's
a blessing that one has to guard lovingly and carefully, but
not anxiously. It's seeing things through the other's eyes,
what does he need now? It's being able to say 'I need you'.
It's giving him a present, not because he needs it but
because I thought of him when I saw it. God gave us
marriage so that we could comfort and help each other; so
that we could encourage each other to face the day and its
difficulties, the work we do separately or together; so that
the person can become what he wants to be, what he is
meant to be – and most of all, so that he can be happy.
Jonathan went to David, it says in the Old Testament, 'and
helped him to find strength in God'. And I know that is
what marriage is about in the end – indeed what all human
relationships are about.

Hanna Ahrens, *Who'd be a Mum!*

Help us as individuals to see the needs of our partners and
friends, and to want to help them in their desire and need to
find you or to know you better.

*

I will praise the Lord, who counsels me. Psalm 16:7

The Lord is my shepherd, I shall lack nothing. He makes me lie down in green pastures, he leads me beside quiet waters, he restores my soul. Psalm 23:1–3

A mother and a wife, so many women are both of these to other people. There are times when they must feel completely submerged in a dual role which somehow fails to recognize them as people.

Our Father in heaven does not do that. Each person is an individual being whom he knows intimately. He knows how we relate to one another because that is a part of his work and he is concerned with the wife/husband relationship as well as the parent/child one, but his love is towards each individual person in a very special way. He looks upon each one as his child, the relationship with each of us is personal and special. In a wonderful sense we are each 'first' with God, just as he must always be first with us.

There are days when being in a relationship with another person may make us feel, as we sometimes say, 'a second class citizen', when our wishes and desires have to be put aside for the benefit of others. Our identity is never forgotten by God. He knows us, loves us – entirely for ourselves.

Thank you for your love which never changes. Forgive me for ever doubting that I am important to you. Keep me faithful in the place and position which you have given me.

*

The Lord is near to all who call on him. Psalm 145:18

Get rid of all bitterness, rage and anger, brawling and slander, along with every form of malice. Be kind and compassionate to one another, forgiving each other, just as in Christ God forgave you. Ephesians 4:31–32

To be a Christian means to forgive others because God forgives us. When we say it like that it seems fairly easy. If someone, having dealt us a heavy blow, asks for forgiveness, we know that we must find that forgiveness and it often is within our capability. It is the small things that we scarcely recognize as needing forgiveness that defeat us – the things within the family group, children who are selfish, husbands who lack understanding, the demanding mother-in-law. Perhaps it is in the office, the boss, with his or her unmannerly ways towards us, the colleagues who leave things undone, or expect us to do more than we consider a fair share of the work.

Do we recognize our need to forgive them? It is not only because it will help us as we consciously accept what is being done to us and deliberately set out to forgive, but because these are the terms that God has set out for us. As we receive forgiveness so we must forgive others. Perhaps we need to have a permanent attitude of refusing to take offence but of showing love and compassion towards others at all times, a realization that we too need continual forgiveness, remembering that God forgives us.

Help me to live in the attitude of love and compassion towards others, remembering that as you forgive me so you desire me to forgive. Make this a permanent attitude in me towards others so that they may see Christ in me and I may please you.

*

He is my loving God and my fortress, my stronghold and my deliverer. Psalm 144:2

Greet Tryphena and Tryphosa, those women who work hard in the Lord. Greet my dear friend Persis, another woman who has worked very hard in the Lord. Romans 16:12

It would be difficult to fault Paul in his general attitude to women, marriage and the family. In his contacts with his hostesses, audiences and female members of his team, he is uniformly chivalrous and brotherly, he never hints or asserts any superiority of men over women. In his letters he expresses the highest regard and esteem for his female colleagues, and commends them as his fellow-workers in the gospel without any discrimination between them and male members of the team. In appraising his attitude and teaching, the cultural climate of his times must be kept in view. One need only compare his outlook and practice with those of the leaders and founders of the other great religions to see the great superiority of his conception of the status of women as compared with that of Buddhism, Hinduism and Islam. Instead of denouncing Paul Christian women should be lauding his championship, for it has paved the way for so many blessings and privileges that they now enjoy.

J. Oswald Sanders, *Paul the Leader*

You created me as a woman, I rejoice in this. Help me to be all that you expect of me.

*

Ascribe to the Lord the glory due to his name. 1 Chronicles 16:29

Dear friends, let us love one another, for love comes from God. Everyone who loves has been born of God and knows God. Whoever does not love does not know God, because God is love. 1 John 4:7–8

In order to spread joy, it is necessary to have joy in one's family. Peace and war begin in the home. If we really want peace in the world, let us first love one another, in the family. We shall then have the joy of Christ, our strength. It is sometimes very hard to smile at one another. It is often hard for the husband to smile on his wife, or for the wife to smile on her husband.

Joy is a net of love by which we can capture souls. God loves the person who gives with joy. Whoever gives with joy gives more. The best way to show our gratitude to God and to people is to accept with joy. Joy can thrive in a heart burning with love.

Mother Teresa, *The Love of Christ*

I want your love to shine through me, Lord, I want to have your joy always in my heart.

*

Sing to the Lord! Give praise to the Lord! Jeremiah 20:13

So Moses brought their case before the Lord and the Lord said to him, 'What Zelophehad's daughters are saying is right. You must certainly give them property as an inheritance among their father's relatives and give their father's inheritance over to them.' Numbers 27:5–7

These five women proved the words of David to be written many years later. 'The Lord is a refuge for the oppressed, a stronghold in times of trouble' (Psalm 9:9). By bringing her difficulties to God, a single woman can avoid self-pity and rebellion, the two dangerous rocks on which the life of the single person most easily runs aground. Throughout the ages women without fathers or husbands to speak for them have lived with disappointment and bitterness. But the daughters of Zelophehad showed there was another way. Not only did they get what they asked for, but others shared their victory. From then on women of Israel in a similar position would have the rights these five gained. With their brave act, the legal hereditary law of daughters was established.

   These five sisters also proved that God doesn't turn a deaf ear to single women. He is concerned with their needs, he loves them and considers their desires if their motives are pure and their aims acceptable.

Gien Karssen, *Getting the Most out of Being Single*

You can be to us all that we need. Single women can prove this by bringing you into that part of life that needs love and companionship. Give those who are alone your guidance and help too, in all the practical things of life which can be such a burden.

*

My mouth will speak in praise of the Lord. Psalm 145:21

Jesus called the children to him and said, 'Let the little children come to me, and do not hinder them, for the kingdom of God belongs to such as these.' Luke 18:16

Man and Satan govern by driving with power from behind. God stands before his creation and woos us in love to respond to him. He draws all animate nature after him by his beautiful presence, evoking obedience by desire – perhaps even inanimate motive, too, who knows? Our privilege as parents is to be caught in this vibrant flow of responsive desire toward God and to awaken the same desires in our children, attacking their hearts till they are drawn by our love and find his also. That is Christian parenthood.

Roger Forster, *We Believe in Marriage*

Bless our children, Lord; may they see you in us and desire you for themselves.

A Break in the Day
The Gift of Salvation

O Lord, you are my God; I will exalt you and praise your name. Isaiah 25:1

And God is able to make all grace abound to you, so that in all things at all times, having all that you need, you will abound in every good work. 2 Corinthians 9:8

The acceptance of ourselves and one another as we are is an important truth, but it may need qualification if it is not to be misunderstood. It is commonly said that God loves us as we are and that that is how we should love our neighbour and ourselves. There is truth in this but it is not the whole truth: for we are living persons and destined to grow in ever fuller measure into the stature of Christ. A man may not love a living thing in the same way that he loves an inanimate object. I love a favourite picture as it is, and shall dust it tomorrow that it may remain as it is today. I have too a favourite plant and I love that too for what it is (at this particular instant), but I shall water it that it may become what now it is not. God's love for us is clearly analogous to a man's love for his plant, and a right love for ourselves follows the same pattern. In accepting ourselves as we are, we acknowledge that this is how God would at this instant have us to be, but we do not forget the continuing watering of his grace which is destined to carry us not simply to where we are not, but beyond any horizons we can now imagine.

Robert Llewelyn, *With Pity not with Blame*

Thank you, Father, that by your grace you are continually working in me. Make me what you want me to be. Thank you too, that you are not impatient at my progress.

*

O Lord, I say to you, 'You are my God.' Psalm 140:6

If you, then, though you are evil, know how to give good gifts to your children, how much more will your Father in heaven give good gifts to those who ask him! Matthew 7:11

In the sermon on the mount Jesus gives us a comprehensive doctrine of God. He is the Creator, the living God of the natural order, who gives sunshine and rain, and supplies birds with food, flowers with clothing and human beings with the necessities of life. He is also the King whose righteous and saving rule has irrupted into human lives through Jesus. But above all – again through Jesus – he is our Father. Addressing his disciples, Jesus constantly referred to him as 'your Father in heaven', whose children they were, whose mercy they must copy, whose loving providence they must trust and to whom they must come confidingly in prayer, knowing that he will never give them anything but 'good gifts'.

John W. Stott, *Christian Counter Culture*

Thank you, Father, for all your good gifts, but especially for the gift of yourself.

*

The Lord is faithful to all his promises. Psalm 145:13

Ascribe to the Lord the glory due to his name; worship the Lord in the splendour of his holiness. Psalm 29:2

Two attitudes in worship are equally applicable. The first is prostration. This gives a sense of being both a creature and unworthy. It is a physical position that acknowledges appropriately the majesty, glory and holy righteousness of God. It states a belief that God is high and exalted, dwelling in a place of burning inextinguishable light; that there is no darkness or inconsistency in what he does and wills; that he is the author of life in all its fullness and destroys all that brings death and chaos. The second attitude is to hold the head high. It means that we can look at God and speak to him face to face as a person speaks to their friend.

Worship is to acknowledge that God is the one who forgives all our rebellions and cleanses us from all our faults, that he is our Father who runs towards us, embraces us as lost children when we return home from the wilderness and casts out all fear from our lives.

Worship is confessing who God is and letting him be God. It is praise to the one from whom all truth, goodness, beauty and harmony flow. It is rejoicing in the work of God's hands. It is joy and confidence in the living God who has conquered death, deceit and doubt and opened up a new world to live in. Above all, worship is loving God with all we are and all we have, making everything available for him.

Andrew Kirk, *A New World Coming*

I bow before you in praise and adoration, my Lord and my God.

*

A Break in the Day

My mouth will speak in praise of the Lord. Psalm 145:21

I have brought you glory on earth by completing the work you gave me to do. John 17:4

There were endless demands on Jesus' time. People pressed on him with their needs so that he and his disciples had not leisure even to eat, and he would go away into the hills to pray and be alone. At times the disciples came to him with reproach because he was not available when needed. There must have been everywhere he went, those who wanted to be healed who could not get to him, because of the crowds, or who learned too late that Jesus of Nazareth was passing by, or who had no one to carry them to him, or to send to ask him to come to them. How many 'if only's' he must have left behind, how much more that he could have done. There must have been things, also, that Jesus himself would have liked to do during those three packed years of his public ministry, but he was a man, with a man's limitation of time and space. Yet he took time to rest, withdrawing to the hills to pray alone and sometimes taking his disciples to lonely places where they were free of the crowds. Still he was able to make that amazing claim 'I have finished the work you gave me to do'. This was not the same as saying he had finished everything he could possibly think of to do or that he had done everything others had asked. He made no claim to have done what he wanted to do. The claim was that he had done what had been *given*.

Elizabeth Elliot, *Discipline – the Glad Surrender*

Show me, Lord, how to use my time to do the things that you want me to do, but help me also not to take on tasks from a misplaced feeling that I should be doing them.

*

Give thanks to the Lord, for he is good. Psalm 136:1

He [Aaron] shall then slaughter the goat for the sin offering for the people. Leviticus 16:15

'Who do you say I am?' Peter answered, 'You are the Christ.' Mark 8:29

We believe that it was this picture which Peter saw in Jesus. He saw Jesus carrying our sins in his own body to the Cross, just as the scapegoat carried the sins of Israel. He believed that if a man with a contrite and penitent heart laid his sins, as it were, on Jesus Christ, Jesus bore them in his own body in his death on the Cross, and thus restored the lost relationship between man and God. To us the ritual may be strange but to a Jew the picture of Jesus as the scapegoat would be very vivid. And this we do know – it was indeed our sins which crucified our Lord, and he in his death found the remedy and cure for them.

William Barclay, *Jesus As They Saw Him*

Thank you, Father, for this picture of Jesus as the scapegoat, taking away my sin, suffering that I might be saved and restored. May I never forget the agony that had to be borne in order that I might walk in freedom and fellowship with you.

*

O Lord, you have searched me and you know me. Psalm 139:1

Remember the Sabbath day by keeping it holy. . . . For in six days the Lord made the heavens and the earth, the sea, and all that is in them, but he rested on the seventh day. Therefore the Lord blessed the Sabbath day and made it holy. Exodus 20:8,11

Recently I read that a family tried to keep Sunday very special. The parents put aside the temptation to do the small jobs that accumulate and relaxed and enjoyed the day.

How easy it is to fill Sunday with something that we think just has to be done – usually something that should have been done the day before, or could just as easily be fitted in on another day. If we obeyed the Lord's command to keep the Sabbath holy, we would not take it into account as a day that we could use for work. Automatically everything would be fitted into the other six days.

On the other hand, I don't think that it should be a melancholy day, but one in which we enjoy the company of family and friends, yet remember that in a special way it is God's day, a day when there is no difficulty in finding some time to spend with him and to go to his house, a day that is very different because he has given it to us in order that it should be so.

I often forget or feel that it is unimportant to keep your special day in the way that you have commanded. Help me to honour it and use it so as to draw even closer to you.

*

Praise be to his glorious name for ever; may the whole earth be filled with his glory. Psalm 72:19

The jailer called for lights, rushed in and fell trembling before Paul and Silas. He then brought them out and asked, 'Men, what must I do to be saved?' They replied, 'Believe in the Lord Jesus, and you will be saved – you and your household.' Acts 16:29–31

To know about Christ is not enough. To be convinced that he is the Saviour of the world is not enough. To affirm your faith in him, as we do in the Apostles' Creed, is not enough. To believe that he has saved others is not enough. You really don't actively believe in Christ until you make a commitment of your life and receive him as your Saviour. You can best demonstrate your faith in a bank by putting your money in it. You can best show your faith in a doctor by trusting him with your physical welfare in times of illness. You can best prove your faith in a boat by getting aboard and going somewhere on it. You can best demonstrate your faith in Christ by trusting him with your life and receiving him unconditionally as your Saviour.

Billy Graham, *The Secret of Happiness*

Lord Jesus, I want every part of my life to be given over to you, because you have done so much for me. Through your death I live, my life is yours. Keep me from wanting to go my own way; may I rejoice in doing your will.

*

Serve the Lord with gladness; come before him with joyful songs. Psalm 100:2

Blessed are the peacemakers, for they will be called sons of God. Matthew 5:9

God calls us as his children to be not peace-loving but peacemakers, which is a different thing. It is not easy. Paul reminds us that 'God made peace [with us] through the death of his own son'. In this torn and troubled world we must be willing to go into tense and difficult situations and do what we can to make peace, with the love of Christ in our hearts and with the power of his Spirit in our lives. Perhaps we need to start in our own homes, with husband and wife, parent or child; or perhaps we need to work for peace in our churches or in our places of work. If in the process we are misunderstood and falsely accused, so was Jesus. In every area of life this peacemaking, reconciling work is most desperately needed today.

David Watson, *Is Anyone There?*

Teach me what it means to be a peacemaker. Show me how to be one in the power of the Holy Spirit so that I may help in the advancement of your kingdom.

*

O Lord, our Lord, how majestic is your name in all the earth! Psalm 8:1

Zacchaeus stood up and said to the Lord, 'Look, Lord! Here and now I give half of my possessions to the poor.' Luke 19:8

If we confess our sins, he is faithful and just and will forgive us our sins and purify us from all unrighteousness. 1 John 1:9

I have a favourite visual illustration of repentance. I turn my back on my visitor and start talking to the wall. After a while, I turn my head and ask him if he is still there. He laughs uncertainly. Eventually I turn right round, face him, and explain, 'I've been doing what we all do to God'. We go our own way. We talk to him on our own terms. Occasionally, especially when in trouble, we turn round and see if he is still there. But what he requires from us is quite different. He wants us to go completely his way. That's what repentance means. And when you've done that, God gives you his Holy Spirit to make the change possible (to be more precise it is the Holy Spirit who has brought you this far; though you don't realize it!). It's not essentially up to you, it's up to him, to keep you in the changed state. Such total repentance will inevitably, like Zacchaeus, include restitution and penitence. And it is lasting and life-giving.

John Woolmer, *Growing up to Salvation*

I praise and thank you for opening my mind to the truth of salvation. Thank you for wanting me and helping me to turn to you and walk in your way.

*

Hosanna! Blessed is he who comes in the name of the Lord!
Mark 11:9

Therefore, if anyone is in Christ, he is a new creation; the
old has gone, the new has come! All this is from God, who
reconciled us to himself through Christ and gave us the
ministry of reconciliation. 2 Corinthians 5:17–18

Christians are called to be reconcilers, bridge people. That
will mean repeatedly making the first move towards understanding and staying with those who feel deeply alienated;
that will often mean being refuted by suspicion or anger. It
may also bring harsh criticisms from those who lay the
blame entirely upon the alienated themselves. We shall be
accused of being soft and of undermining society. Some
may see that as would-be reconcilers they will be attacked
from both sides, yet refuse to give up the attempt; they may
come to perceive that beneath the will to bring about reconciliation lies the deep experience of the human heart of
knowing what it is to be reconciled to God.

David Sheppard, *Bias to the Poor*

Take away my prejudices and show me how I can truly
undertake the work of reconciliation as you show it to us in
your Word.

*

I am God, and there is none like me. Isaiah 46:9

'Love the Lord your God with all your heart and with all your soul and with all your mind.' This is the first and greatest commandment. And the second is like it: 'Love your neighbour as yourself.' Matthew 22:37–39

There are only two duties that our Lord requires of us: the love of God, and the love of our neighbour. And, in my opinion, the surest sign for our discovering our love to God is discovering our love to our neighbour. Be assured that the further you advance in the love of your neighbour, the more you are advancing in the love of God.

But alas, many worms lie gnawing at the roots of our love to our neighbour! Self-love, self-esteem, fault-finding, envy, anger, impatience, and scorn.

My sisters, our Lord expects works. Therefore when you see anyone sick, have compassion upon her as if she were yourself. Pity her. Fast that she may eat. Wake that she may sleep.

Again, when you hear anyone commended in praise, rejoice in it as much as if you were commended and praised yourself. This indeed should be easier because where true humility is, praise is prompted. Cover also your sister's defects as you would cover and not expose your own defects and faults.

As often as an occasion offers, lift up your neighbour's burden. Take it from her heart and put it upon yourself.

St Teresa of Avila, *A Life of Prayer*

May I have the mind of my Saviour, the love of my God and the ability in the power of the Spirit to serve you as you desire in every part of my life.

*

A Break in the Day

I am the Lord, and there is no other. Isaiah 45:6

Come to me, all you who are weary and burdened, and I will give you rest. Take my yoke upon you and learn from me, for I am gentle and humble in heart, and you will find rest for your souls. For my yoke is easy and my burden is light. Matthew 11:28–30

The Lord is my pacesetter
    I shall not rush.
He makes me to stop
    for quiet intervals.
He provides me with images of stillness
    which restore my serenity.
He leads me in the ways of efficiency
    through calmness of mind,
        and his guidance
            is peace.
Even though I have a great many things
    to accomplish each day
        I will not fret
            for his presence is here.
His timelessness,
    his all-importance
        will keep me in balance.
He prepares refreshment
    in the midst of my activity
        by anointing my mind
            with his oil of tranquillity.
My cup of joyous energy overflows.
    Surely harmony and effectiveness
        shall be the fruit of my hours,

And I shall walk
   in the pace of the Lord
      and dwell in his house
         forever.

                          Author unknown

I know I keep going when really you want me to be still with you, Lord. Please help me not only to manage my time, but also show me the priorities in my life. I do long to have you minister to me; enable me to be quiet so that I can hear you speak, but also that we may be silent together.

*

God is our refuge and strength, an ever present help in trouble. Psalm 46:1

God loves a cheerful giver. 2 Corinthians 9:7

This service that you perform is not only supplying the needs of God's people but is also overflowing in many expressions of thanks to God. 2 Corinthians 9:12

It sometimes annoys me when I give a gift to another who in turn gives it away. What a waste, I think, I could have kept it for myself. When the Spirit prompts us to give – in money or in kind – and we think that the money is badly spent or the object not appreciated, we are tempted to think that it has been wasted. But our responsibility finishes when we have been obedient and fulfilled the request that we feel has been made to us by God.

Whether it is our regular tithe or a gift of thanks over and above that, our Father is concerned with the way we give. The gift is to him and having given it with a thankful heart and in joy we should then forget it; we should refuse to allow the thought that our money may have been badly used to enter our head. In fact it may have been well used in a way we cannot understand, but in any case the responsibility is not ours if we have been obedient.

May I learn the joy of obedience that delights in doing your will in exactly the way you ask.

*

Let them give thanks to the Lord for his unfailing love and his wonderful deeds for men. Psalm 107:15

Then a great and powerful wind tore the mountains apart and shattered the rocks before the Lord, but the Lord was not in the wind. After the wind there was an earthquake, but the Lord was not in the earthquake. After the earthquake came a fire, but the Lord was not in the fire. And after the fire came a gentle whisper. 1 Kings 19:11–12

When we speak of 'listening' to God we are talking about a listening of the spirit, a tuning of our inmost being to 'hear' the word of God. By 'the word of God' I mean not only the actual written words of the Scriptures but God's message in all its manifestations. God 'speaks' to us through the Scriptures, through the events in our lives, through the people we meet, through history, through nature – through everything. But, as in ordinary physical listening, we must keep silence if we are to hear what God is saying to us. Sometimes, of course, he will speak to people in such a manner that they cannot fail to hear – as, for instance, he spoke to Saul of Tarsus, in an encounter so violent that it knocked Saul off his horse and blinded him. . . . Most people, like the prophet Elijah, find that God speaks very quietly. . . . Just as Elijah recognized that God was speaking to him not in the wind or the earthquake but in the gentle breeze, we have to learn to hear him in the quiet of our soul and in the ordinary events of our day.

Sheila Cassidy, *Prayer for Pilgrims*

Lord, please give me a listening heart, that I may go through each day not only expecting you to speak to me but alert to catch your whisper. May my heart be obedient, set to obey you in all things in response to your word.

Help Me, Lord

My Life is Yours

Give thanks to the Lord, for he is good. Psalm 107:1

Some men came carrying a paralytic on a mat and tried to take him into the house to lay him before Jesus. When they could not find a way to do this because of the crowd, they went up on the roof and lowered him on his mat through the tiles into the middle of the crowd, right in front of Jesus. Luke 5: 18–19

We should never be alone when we suffer. I don't mean never for a moment, or that we must not live in an apartment by ourselves. But we should never build a self-imposed wall around us that allows absolutely no one inside to see what we're going through and to hurt with our hurts. God never intended that we shoulder the load of suffering by ourselves. If you are single or widowed, you may feel as though such an intimate sharing of sorrows is impossible. But you do have a family – other Christians, the body of Christ. This family of believers is meant to be one of the warmest and most intimate circles of friendship in the world, I believe, and am told by my married friends, that even for a married person it is a mistake to try and rely on one's partner as one's total source of fellowship. God deliberately designed the Church to consist of young and old, male and female, all types of people, and we need to rub shoulders with them all if our innermost needs are to be met.

Joni Eareksen and Steve Estes, *A Step Further*

Be with those who suffer, Father, and give them the ability to turn to others for help, knowing that you work through people. Help me to know how to comfort and encourage those in need, and not to begrudge the time or the effort it may take.

*

I will praise the Lord all my life. Psalm 146:2

And this is the testimony: God has given us eternal life, and this life is in his Son. He who has the Son has life; he who does not have the Son of God does not have life. I write these things to you who believe in the name of the Son of God so that you may know that you have eternal life. 1 John 5:11–13

Our experience of grief will be conditioned by how much the resources of the Christian faith are ours. The Christian knows that death is not the end, even for the body. Those who die as Christians will be raised with a new and glorious body like Jesus' resurrection body. The resources of the resurrection help us to think of the person as we know him. In addition we treat the body with respect.

The Christian knows that death is not the end for the inner person. The spirit of one who has died 'in Christ' does not die, but rather goes to be with the Lord, which Paul says 'is far better'.

All who have faith in Jesus Christ can know the strength of his presence, helping them to deal with grief and, when the time comes, to face death itself.

Harold Bauman, *Living Through Grief*

Father – I do not fear death, but the pathway of death. You have said that your grace is sufficient. Thank you for the strength to believe that this grace will support me when the time of need comes; when I know the loss of one who walks that pathway or when the time comes to start along it myself.

*

The Lord delights in those who fear him, who put their hope in his unfailing love. Psalm 147:11

But Jonah was greatly displeased and became angry. He prayed to the Lord, 'O Lord, is this not what I said when I was still at home? That is why I was so quick to flee to Tarshish. I knew that you are a gracious and compassionate God, slow to anger and abounding in love, a God who relents from sending calamity. Now, O Lord, take away my life, for it is better for me to die than to live.' Jonah 4: 1–3

It is a comfort to remember that the greatness of God's love is such that if we need to vent our feelings of anger and let down to him, we can do so. It is right that we do this rather than push them down into ourselves or transform them into emotions of bitterness. We shall not be punished for exposing negative feelings towards God. We do not have to come to him on our best behaviour or in our party dress. He wants to meet with us as we are. If this means coming sometimes with anger and fury, he is big enough to contain this. His constant loving of us is of such a quality that it will not stop because of our invectives. It is better for us to get our wretched feelings out rather than repress them. God even wants our apparently unacceptable feelings. He wants the lot!

Margaret Evening, *Who Walk Alone*

I sometimes shout and get angry with you, Father, and yet I realize even as I do it that the moment will come when I have to say, 'Please forgive me'. Thank you for being with me at all times, for your understanding and love. Help me to learn from you so that my thoughts may more often follow yours, and that I may find joy in wanting only your will.

*

Sing of the ways of the Lord, for the glory of the Lord is great. Psalm 138:5

'I know the plans I have for you,' declares the Lord, 'plans to prosper you and not to harm you, plans to give you hope and a future.' Jeremiah 29:11

As life on the dole began, bitter resentment festered in me against those I blamed for such upheaval and degradation in our lives. When I read 'Bless those who curse you, pray for those who ill treat you' I closed the Bible quickly. I could not, I would not. But the Holy Spirit kept prompting those words until I realized an act of will was required – if I would, then I could. 'Father, I will pray for them. . . .

90

Bless them.' As I said those words I felt different. The root of bitterness was out. Concern and forgiveness began to grow, then healing properties bringing inner release.

Diana Peck, *Decision Magazine*

How do I know that I have faith unless it is tested, Father? I do believe, help me overcome my unbelief – this is my prayer.

*

Look to the Lord and his strength; seek his face always. Psalm 105:4

I consider everything a loss compared to the surpassing greatness of knowing Christ Jesus my Lord, for whose sake I have lost all things. I consider them rubbish, that I may gain Christ and be found in him. Philippians 3:8–9

Though we are in such pain, trouble and distress, that it seems as though we are unable to think of anything except how we are and what we feel, yet as soon as we may, we are to pass lightly over it, and count it as nothing. And why? Because God wills that we should understand that if we know him and love him and reverently fear him, we shall have rest and be at peace. And we shall rejoice in all that he does.

Julian of Norwich, *Enfolded in Love*

It is so difficult to accept what you have planned for us, Father. Help me to learn to think as you do. To fret and grumble less and concentrate more on you as one who loves me and whom I long to love more and more.

*

Ascribe to the Lord the glory due to his name. Psalm 96:8

But one thing I do: Forgetting what is behind and straining towards what is ahead, I press on towards the goal to win the prize for which God has called me heavenwards in Christ Jesus. Philippians 3:13–14

The best piece of advice that I was ever given has been remembered over very many years: When you fall, pick yourself up and go on! There have been times when having done something stupid, acted badly, hurt others, it has felt just like falling into darkness. The quicker I have taken myself in hand, scrambled up, made it right with God and started off again the better it has been. Lying in the mud of self-pity never really helped.

Father, you know the times that I harden my heart against you. Make me teachable so that I may learn more and more to please you, both in my attitudes and in the way in which I conduct my life. I want my eyes to be continually fixed on the prize in Jesus Christ.

*

Praise, O servants of the Lord, praise the name of the Lord.
Psalm 113:1

For God so loved the world that he gave his one and only
Son, that whoever believes in him shall not perish but have
eternal life. John 3:16

How many people, facing the thought of the death of a
loved one, have found that when God is allowed into the
circumstance they come to realize that his love for that
person is greater even than their own and that he can
support and comfort them in their sorrow? If we harden our
hearts in the face of any distress, we suffer more. When we
turn away from God, the pain appears greater. As we long
only to share the sorrows – and the joys – of our children, so
our 'Abba' longs to do the same. We so often fail to remember that he allowed his Son to suffer, and to understand how
he must have felt as he watched him go through such pain.
But because he did, we know too that he must love us very
much, and the one who truly loves always suffers with the
object of his love. We find that he does more than share,
that he is drawing us into a deeper spiritual relationship. In
the end we can even be glad of the loss and suffering, for we
know that the experience had to be gone through in order to
find something so wonderful.

Father, so often it is when the dark times are over that I
realize how close you have been. Keep me always aware of
your concern and love so that I may be able to praise you
when I am going through the darkness, and that I may be
able to see with the eyes of faith the light at the end of the
tunnel.

*

Give thanks to him and praise his name. Psalm 100:4

For God, who said, 'Let light shine out of darkness', made his light shine in our hearts to give us the light of the knowledge of the glory of God in the face of Christ. But we have this treasure in jars of clay to show that this all-surpassing power is from God and not from us. 2 Corinthians 4:6–7

It lifts the tension or the disappointment and brings some relief in the midst of frustration or despair, if we remember that we have been given, in ten-foot-high letters, brightened by a spotlight, the fact that we are not to expect anything like perfection now. We are 'earthen vessels' made up of chippable, breakable and crackable earth. The promises of perfection are for a time ahead. Right now we are to have a very specialized opportunity, that of holding within us and giving out to others the priceless treasures of truth as opposed to falsehood, light as opposed to darkness, knowledge as opposed to ignorance. Our own cracks, chips, wobbly handles and marred beauty are not in any way to detract from the perfection and wonder of the 'excellency' or greatness of the power of God.

Edith Schaeffer, *Affliction*

How often, Lord, can I only think of my unworthiness, see where I have marred and damaged the clay which is my life. Yet you have entrusted to your children the marvellous treasure of the Gospel. Keep me faithful in revealing this good news to others.

*

Help Me, Lord

Great is our Lord and mighty in power. Psalm 147:5

For we do not have a high priest who is unable to sympathize with our weaknesses, but we have one who has been tempted in every way, just as we are – yet was without sin. Hebrews 4:15

We cannot truly enter into the sorrows, pains and humiliations of others without having ourselves gone through some such suffering. We have to work through our own pains by going to others to open our grief! If we are not prepared to do this because of pride or fear, we will have little chance of rapport with others in their suffering, nor indeed will we be the type of person to whom they feel they can open their hearts. We cannot lead others where we have not been. Further, if we have been unwilling to enter into our own pain, we shall not see the necessity for others to enter into theirs, nor indeed, shall we be able to show them how this is possible.

The reason Christ can enter into our sufferings and lead us to share those of others is that he felt human pain without reserve in his own flesh. When *we* have suffered in our flesh, we can know what it is to stay and share with others, as they agonize with loud cries and tears in reliving their dread, desolation, rage and confusion.

Reginald East, *Heal the Sick*

Jesus, you healed many people when here on earth, and we may still look to you for healing. Lord, I pray that I may learn how to help others, to listen when they speak, to bring them to you for the healing they may need. Take away any fear I may have, only make me of use day by day.

*

For I am the Lord, your God, who takes hold of your right hand and says to you, Do not fear. Isaiah 41:13

The Lord will guide you always; he will satisfy your needs in a sun-scorched land and will strengthen your frame. You will be like a well-watered garden, like a spring whose waters never fail. Isaiah 58:11

Loneliness is a very complex thing. Being alone is not of itself loneliness, we all need to be alone at times. It is in the times of being alone that we get to know ourselves, which can be for our good.

True loneliness is difficult and painful because it sometimes means having to face up to the reason why we are lonely. It could mean that we find it difficult to give out to other people, to respond to their overtures. We may not have an attractive personality, we may even resent our place in society, too little money, a lack of background, or alternatively, money and many of the good things of life which we have come to accept as our due put up a barrier which we keep in place.

Loneliness can come from not being satisfied with oneself as a person, or feeling inferior, or not having accomplished in life what others appear to have done so easily. Loneliness can be the pain of so many unanswered questions. Loneliness is feeling unloved and unwanted. It is sometimes a part of guilt or a result of pride. It may be that all those near to us have already died.

God has said that he will never leave us, so we may be sure of his continual presence. If we refuse to bring him fully into every part of our life then here is an additional cause of feeling alone. He has said that he will satisfy us. Do we believe that he can fulfil all that he says?

Dear Father, in you is all that I need in the fullest possible sense. Help me to look to you for my understanding of this, so that I may show by my life that you are faithful to your word.

*

God made the earth by his power. Jeremiah 10:12

The Lord himself goes before you and will be with you; he will never leave you nor forsake you. Do not be afraid; do not be discouraged. Dueteronomy 31:8

I once read of a man whose life was marked by hardship. He was a Christian, but life was not easy. One loss followed another, and disappointment and pain seemed to be his closest friends. One night he had a dream. He was with the Lord looking back on his life, which was portrayed as footprints along a sandy beach. Usually there were two sets of footprints – his and the Saviour's. But as he looked closer, he saw only one set of footprints along the very rugged places. He frowned, confused, and asked the Lord: 'Look there. You and I have walked together during much of my lifetime . . . but when things got really bad, where'd you go? I needed you at those times more than ever. Why'd you leave?' The answer came, 'My child, I have never left you. The two sets of footprints assure you of that. But there were times when it was almost more than you could bear. At those very, very hard times, I carried you in my arms. The single set of footprints you see at those perilous places are mine. It was when I was carrying you.' We may feel alone, forsaken and forgotten but we are not. In times of loss our God picks us up and holds us close.

Charles Swindoll, *Three Steps Forward, Two Steps Back*

Lord Jesus, thank you for your great love for me. Don't let me forget your continued presence or the realization of it.

*

Let everything that has breath praise the Lord. Psalm 150:6

Shout for joy, O heavens; rejoice, O earth; burst into song, O mountains! For the Lord comforts his people and will have compassion on his afflicted ones.

But Zion said, 'The Lord has forsaken me, the Lord has forgotten me.' Can a mother forget the baby at her breast and have no compassion on the child she has borne? Though she may forget, I will not forget you! See, I have engraved you on the palms of my hands. Isaiah 49:13–16

Sometimes in the midst of a normal day, doing everyday things, a feeling of complete loss, emptiness, aloneness can come with the suddenness of a clap of thunder. All the hurts ever experienced flood in overwhelmingly, any rejection is felt again like a sudden blow. It is impossible to know why the feeling of desolation comes, why a life that is happy and satisfying suddenly seems to melt away, and only despair remains. Only when we make the deliberate effort of turning to God and allowing the mind to take hold of the certainties that we know of him will the waves of pain recede and peace and calmness return. The longer we wallow in the sense of despair, the longer our anguish and the more we must grieve the One who loves us and wants to help. To be known as God knows us should be encouragement enough to help us through the darkest hours.

Dear Lord, may the knowledge of your love and the promises found in your Word sustain all who go through times of despair. When I am tempted by such moods of darkness help me to turn quickly to you, to find the strength that I need to break free and to go on, secure in the knowledge of your caring.

*

Sing praises to God, sing praises. Psalm 47:6

Do not conform any longer to the pattern of this world, but be transformed by the renewing of your mind. Romans 12:2

We claim as Christians that the centre of our life has been shifted from ourselves to Christ – yet some of us are chronically selfish still. We say that the first of all the graces is humility – but we are proud. We talk of 'a peace that passes all understanding' – yet we are restless within, and our inner restlessness betrays itself in a lack of response. We claim to be 'children of the heavenly King' – but we feel inferior. We say that from the heart of the Christian perfect love has cast out fear – but we are as fearful as the next man. Daily we pray that we may be forgiven our trespasses 'as we forgive those who trespass against us' – yet we harbour resentments and are not strangers to bitterness. There is no joy like the joy of a Christian 'we have said' – but we are moody. We complain over trifles, are sometimes guilty of meanness, and time and time again are negative in our thought.

W. E. Sangster, *The Secret of a Radiant Life*

Father, forgive me when I fail you by being so much less than I should be. Fill me with your Holy Spirit that I may show by my life that I belong to you.

*

I love you, O Lord, my strength. Psalm 18:1

Trust in the Lord with all your heart and lean not on your own understanding; in all your ways acknowledge him, and he will make your paths straight. Proverbs 3:5–6

I realized that although I had met Jesus and knew him to be the answer I could not compel the children to accept this truth second hand. I could only pray that my Lord would open their eyes; and I took comfort in the words from Proverbs 22:6, 'Teach a child to choose the right way and when he is older he will remain upon it.' It does not say that the growing child, the adolescent, even the grown man, won't try many wrong paths before he returns to the right one, but it does give the assurance that he will return to the right one in the end. And as I looked back over the years I had tried to make it without the Lord, I saw that Jesus had been there all the time, gently jogging my life along, keeping me afloat, preventing disasters and waiting patiently in the wings for me to realize my own helplessness – and admit it.

Noreen Riols, *Eye of the Storm*

Lord, cause my eyes to be continually fixed on you so that I may not be tempted to turn aside into my own way.

*

Many, O Lord my God, are the wonders you have done. Psalm 40:5

He said to them, 'How foolish you are, and how slow of heart to believe all that the prophets have spoken! Did not the Christ have to suffer these things and then enter his glory?' And beginning with Moses and all the Prophets, he explained to them what was said in all the Scriptures concerning himself. Luke 24:25–27

There are numerous examples throughout his public ministry where Jesus counsels people – the frustrated invalid, the social snob, the petty protectionist, the crooked civil servant, the pillar of the establishment, the man of means, and so many who came to him for healing, such as the woman in the crowd who touched him and the blind beggar who cried to him. He even counselled a dying criminal and brought him healing and salvation. And as the resurrected Lord, he cured the depression of the pair on the way to Emmaus. He counselled families, as he did Martha, whom he believed was concerned with the trivial and petty things of this life, and brought succour and support to the Bethany family in the hour of greatest grief when Lazarus died. He even counselled his disciples when faced with a mass of thousands. Five thousand followed him one day out to the secret retreat in the wilderness. When the disciples begged him to send them away, he demanded that they gave them to eat because he saw them as sheep without a shepherd 'And I love them'. He counselled the disciples again when they were in a state of panic one night on the murderous sea, when they believed that as he slept he cared not that they might perish. Jesus calmed the waves and calmed their anxieties.

His word and counsel created the world; his word and counsel sustains it. His word brings peace, healing and salvation.

M. David Enoch, *Healing the Hurt Mind*

So many people are hurt, Lord. Draw near and help and counsel your children. Enable me to learn from you how to give comfort to others and to be sensitive to their need.

*

Great peace have they who love your law, and nothing can make them stumble. Psalm 119:165

A man with leprosy came to him and begged him on his knees, 'If you are willing, you can make me clean.' Filled with compassion, Jesus reached out his hand and touched the man. 'I am willing,' he said. Mark 1:40–41

Our Lord nearly always brought healing through touch. It was his way of expressing his love and oneness with the sick person. It is not always enough to say all is well, we have to show it too. So often we withdraw physically from the sick, the dying or the disturbed. A mother of a handicapped child told me how much pleasure it gave her when a friend's child hugged her daughter and held her misshapen hands.

Jane Davies, *The Price of Loving*

I should like to look on all your creatures in the same way as you do, Lord, so that where on a human level I might want to turn away, your love in me would enable me to understand and say and do the right thing.

*

Praise our God, all you his servants. Revelation 19:5

While he was by the lake, one of the synagogue rulers, named Jairus, came there. Seeing Jesus, he fell at his feet and pleaded earnestly with him. Mark 5:21–23

'Dear Lord Jesus, be there, in that cubicle. Please be there. May your glory shine around him, your unseen yet felt presence. Oh give Jon your peace, give the doctor your skill, give the nurse your compassion, and oh Lord, may that drug be completely in your control. Oh use it to do Jon good and take away all the harmful side effects. May your healing power stream forth into him and make him whole.' It was the final prayer. This time the Lord answered in full. On this appointed day at this appointed hour, known to the Father from the depths of eternity, Almighty God displayed to us his omnipotence and his mercy and his love. Our brave child Jonathan was lifted up from that bed of suffering, released from life, snatched in an instant from the world, to be received into the awaiting and welcoming and loving embrace of his Lord Jesus healed, whole, safe for evermore.

Carol Oldham, *A Child Loaned*

O Father, you answer our call in different ways – but if we are careful to rest in you, you prepare us for the answer, so that when it comes we can accept it. Keep me resting in you, so that whatever comes I may be able to bear it.

*

The Lord has done great things for us, and we are filled with joy. Psalm 126:3

Praise the Lord, O my soul. O Lord my God, you are very great; you are clothed with splendour and majesty. He wraps himself in light as with a garment; he stretches out the heavens like a tent. Psalm 104:1–2

Reading the Psalms we catch a glimpse of what it means to praise the Lord. The range of thought and the language in which the greatness of God is described are the widest and the most powerful which the human mind and heart can achieve. We may find it difficult to lift our minds and thoughts; we tend to be earthbound, and often our praise becomes thanksgiving, which of course is good but concentrates on what God gives rather than on God as a person.

When we are able to meditate on him, and allow our thoughts to rest in wonder on who he is, then our hearts will unfold into that paean of praise that truly glorifies our God.

Enable me to raise my hymn of praise to your glory, O Lord. Make my heart concentrate on you that I may offer you the worship that is your due.

At the Close of the Day
Resting on God's Promises

Great is the Lord, and most worthy of praise. Psalm 48:1

Since, then, you have been raised with Christ, set your hearts on things above, where Christ is seated at the right hand of God. Set your minds on things above, not on earthly things. For you died, and your life is now hidden with Christ in God. Colossians 3:1–3

The life hid with Christ in God is a hidden life, as to its source, but it must not be hidden as to its practical results. People must see that we walk as Christ walked; if we say that we are abiding in him, we must prove that we 'possess' that which we 'profess'. We must, in short, be real followers of Christ and not theoretical ones only. And this means a great deal. It means that we must really and absolutely turn our backs on everything that is contrary to the perfect will of God. It means that we are to be a 'peculiar people' not only in the eyes of God, but in the eyes of the world around us, and that, wherever we go, it will be known from our habits, our tempers, our conversation and our pursuits, that we are followers of the Lord Jesus Christ and are not of the world, even as he was not of the world. We must no longer look upon our money as our own, but as belonging to the Lord, to be used in his service. We must not feel at liberty to use our energies exclusively in the pursuits of worldly means but must recognize that, if we seek first the Kingdom of God and his righteousness, all needful things shall be added unto us.

> Hannah Pearsall Smith,
> *The Christians' Secret of a Happy Life*

Thank you for my salvation. Please help me to understand more and more what it means in terms of no longer living for myself but following your plan for my life. Make me teachable, so that I become more like Christ and others may see that I belong to him.

*

Give thanks to the Lord, call on his name. Isaiah 12:4

I am he, I am he who will sustain you. I have made you and I will carry you; I will sustain you . . . Isaiah 46:4

The very best thing an older person can do is to admit 'I'm getting older. And I have something to offer just like I am!' I appreciate this comment by one woman: 'The happiest day of my life was when I stopped trying to look twenty years younger than I am and decided to be myself. There's a special beauty God has given my silver hair!' That's the best compliment you can pay yourself. Just live with the fact that you are as old as you are. And ask God to keep you alive, charming and 'in touch'.

> Charles Swindoll, *Strike the Original Match*

Cause me, Father, to rejoice in my circumstances and in what I am, for these are what you have planned for me.

*

Praise be to the Lord, the God of Israel, from everlasting to everlasting. Psalm 106:48

Immediately the cock crowed the second time. Then Peter remembered the word Jesus had spoken to him: 'Before the rooster crows twice you will disown me three times.' And he broke down and wept. Mark 14:72

Perhaps it is our circumstances which are felt to be narrow and frustrating. We never had the opportunities which seem to have come the way of other people. Or perhaps some malignant fate has struck at us or those we love, bringing disease or death or some other disaster. Or perhaps nothing much has gone wrong externally but we feel strongly within ourselves that life is hostile and threatening. We see it in the behaviour of other people towards us which appears indifferent or harsh. Or we see it in the state of the world where nations and groups and classes are fighting desperately for their own interests without thought for others. Or worst of all, we see it in the contradictions of our own nature which never allows us to be the sort of people we want to be. And although we can't help this, there is none the less a hanging judge within us always determined to condemn us and, if possible, to stifle, or at least to hide, much of what we are.

It is in the darkness of this kind that Christ brings us light. He assures us that whatever else may be against us, even if we are against ourselves, God, the most real of all realities, is on our side, not condemning us but taking our part and seeing us through.

H. A. Williams, *The True Wilderness*

I need your forgiveness, Father, for thinking that I should be different from what I am. Help me to accept myself, and to remember the working of your Holy Spirit in me. Enable me to depend on him for each new day and to learn from him, that I may grow in my spiritual life.

*

I will extol the Lord at all times. Psalm 34:1

When he saw the crowds, he had compassion on them, because they were harassed and helpless, like sheep without a shepherd. Then he said to his disciples, 'The harvest is plentiful but the workers are few.' Matthew 9:36–37

'A passion for souls', as a former generation termed the compassion believers should have for their fellows, is rare in our day. The great mass of Christian people appear to feel not the slightest responsibility for the eternal welfare of their fellow men. The thought that they are their brother's keeper never seems to cross their minds. If they can ensure their own future, that is the extent of their concern.

J. Oswald Sanders, Effective Evangelism

Father, I dare not ask for others to do what I am not willing also to do. Give me the willingness to talk to others about Jesus, and grant me something of the compassion for others that is his.

*

Great is his love towards us and the faithfulness of the Lord endures for ever. Psalm 117:2

It is because of him that you are in Christ Jesus, who has become for us wisdom from God – that is, our righteousness, holiness and redemption. 1 Corinthians 1:30

If we understood more the love of God, our trust and faith would be much strengthened. Julian of Norwich says, 'Some of us believe that God is all powerful and may do everything; and that he is all wise and can do everything; but as for believing that he is all love, and will do everything, there we hold back.'

Yet it was because of God's love for us that the great plan of salvation for his people in need was put into action, and he came in Jesus to execute it. It is because of God's love that the application of his Son's sacrifice may be applied to us. Our righteousness means having a restored relationship with God; holiness is the continued right relationship, and redemption is freedom from the consequence of past sin. If we can believe in a death, prompted by love, which gives the believer freedom and forgiveness, how is it that we fail to understand that it is the same love which longs to enter more fully into the life it has saved, and will do everything for us? And perhaps even more strange, how is it that we so often fail to respond by giving the whole of our love in return?

Often I think that although you can do all things you are not willing to do anything for me. Forgive me, I ask, and give me a true understanding of your love for me.

*

God is our refuge and strength, an ever present help in trouble. Psalm 146:1

He was despised and rejected by men, a man of sorrows, and familiar with suffering. Like one from whom men hide their faces he was despised, and we esteemed him not. Isaiah 53:3

> When Jesus came to Golgotha they hanged him on a tree.
> They drove great nails through hands and feet, and made
> a Calvary.
> They crowned him with a crown of thorns, red were his
> wounds and deep,
> For those were crude and cruel days, and human flesh
> was cheap.

When Jesus came to Birmingham they simply passed
    him by,
They never hurt a hair of him, they only let him die;
For men had grown more tender, and they would not
    give him pain.
They only just passed down the street, and left him in the
    rain.

Still Jesus cried, 'Forgive them, for they know not what
    they do',
And still it rained the wintry rain that drenched him
    through and through:
The crowds went home and left the streets, without a
    soul to see.
And Jesus crouched against a wall and cried for Calvary.
          G. A. Studdert Kennedy, *The Unutterable Beauty*

I pray for the ability to show by my life that I belong to you.
I pray for the words that will tell that I know you died for
    me.
I pray that through me the Holy Spirit may touch hearts
    that will turn to you.

*

O Lord, you are great, and your name is mighty in power.
Jeremiah 10:6

But because of his great love for us, God, who is rich in
mercy, made us alive with Christ even when we were dead

in transgressions – it is by grace you have been saved. Ephesians 2:4–5

A great many people resent the declared fact that they can do absolutely nothing to reconcile themselves to God, however hard they try. Human pride is intensely hostile to the fact that God himself has effected the reconciliation of the world to himself through Christ. People hate to think that no amount of good works or even self-sacrifice can win or deserve God's favour. Forgiveness, acceptance, restoration (whatever we call it) is a *gift*. There are famous people who have put it on record that the one thing they could not accept about Christianity was its starting point, the acceptance of God's forgiveness. In the end, however, each man or woman has to reach the same conclusion. We are all sinners who need the grace and restoration of God's free forgiveness.

Through the Year with J. B. Phillips

Thank you, Lord, for the gift of forgiveness. Enable me to live in praise and thanksgiving to you.

*

Worship the Lord in the splendour of his holiness. Psalm 96:9

Which of you, if his son asks for bread, will give him a stone? Or if he asks for a fish, will give him a snake? Matthew 7:9–10

My son desires a bicycle. We hear of nothing else but this desire, and we shall certainly give him one – when he is old enough to cope with it. What are we continually asking God for? A spiritual gift? A special job? Perhaps, although not aware of it now, we really could not cope. Later, with other arts learnt, new perspectives, will be the right moment. Then, we shall be ready to use the gift, do the job. There will be much more satisfaction and joy in the bicycle when it comes at the right time to be able to be used and controlled without any fears. Our heavenly Father knows exactly the right time when we too can cope with our bicycle!

Forgive me for my impatience when I ask for something that I feel I want immediately. Basically, I do know that your timing is always just right, and that you know what is best for me.

*

O Lord, open my lips, and my mouth will declare your praise. Psalm 51:15

O Jerusalem, Jerusalem, you who kill the prophets and stone those sent to you, how often I have longed to gather your children together, as a hen gathers her chicks under her wings, but you were not willing! Luke 13:34

Two things puzzle us about God's grief over his people. In the first place we find it hard to believe that God should be upset about our materialism. We are also puzzled that God should feel the pain of desertion. He is self-sufficient, infinite. He has no needs. He pours out riches without lessening anything of what he has or is. There is nothing we can contribute which will add a jot to him. Yet he pleads, feels pain, cries out with longing. Cries to a church that has shielded herself from his pain, a church that refuses to look into his weeping eyes or that feels a strange emptiness where love once burned. If there is a wonder greater than God reduced to a helpless infant in a barn, it is the wonder of an infinite God torn with an agony of longing for a people who have forsaken him and that have no awareness of his pain.

John White, *The Golden Cow*

I think we as your people do grieve you very much over our attitudes. We want material things and forget that in other parts of your world others of your people are in need. Open my mind and heart to their needs.

*

The Sovereign Lord is my strength. Habakkuk 3:19

I, even I, am he who blots out your transgressions, for my own sake, and remembers your sins no more. Isaiah 43:25

Father,
forgive me the petty sins
of a working day.
Forgive the curt remarks,
the mean self-interest
that misses opportunities
for caring, sharing, loving.

Lord,
as you do not bear grudges
against me,
let me not bear grudges
against anyone.
As you do not cling
to the memory of my sins,
let me forget
the wrongs I have suffered.

Father,
forgive us our trespasses
as we forgive those
who trespass against us.

Frank Topping, *The Words of Christ*

Cause me to be able to forgive when it is needed, and also to forget. To remember how you love and forgive me, and to help and encourage others instead of worrying about their attitude towards me.

*

Praise be to the God and Father of our Lord Jesus. Ephesians 1:3

Never be lacking in zeal, but keep your spiritual fervour, serving the Lord. Be joyful in hope, patient in affliction, faithful in prayer. Romans 12:11–12

If you get discouraged because you can't get people to see what you see and do what you do and go as fast as you go, remember what Jesus did. He worked with those who meant business. He started with what he had, and he began where he was. Discouragement comes when you try to start with what you wish you had but don't have, and it intensifies when you insist on trying to be in a position you are not in and probably never will be in. So press on, pour out and serve the Lord with gladness.

Stuart Briscoe, *Bound for Joy*

Sometimes I'm impatient, Lord, with those who appear to be spiritually lethargic. Help me to keep my eyes fixed on you and to follow you and your purposes for my life. Keep me serving you with gladness.

*

O Lord, our Lord, how majestic is your name in all the earth! Psalm 8:9

The Spirit of the Lord is on me, because he has anointed me to preach good news to the poor. He has sent me to proclaim freedom for the prisoners and recovery of sight for the blind, to release the oppressed, to proclaim the year of the Lord's favour. Luke 4:18–19

We are called to bring hope to the humiliated, healing and sight to the broken and blind, freedom to those who are enslaved, release to those imprisoned in the depths of their own mind, and to recall all men to God's unfailing love by showing him to the world in our own lives. According to the urgency with which a religion transmits this summons in the lives of its believers, so it is judged in the world of eternal values. Its concern must be universal in sympathy so that no one is left outside the redemptive love of God. It must also free man from the illusion of dependence on any object, whether material or physical, until his soul finds its eternal rest in God alone.

Martin Israel, Smouldering Fire

Forgive me that I am so concerned with myself. Fill me with your Holy Spirit.

*

Exalt the Lord our God and worship at his footstool; he is holy. Psalm 99:5

Listen to me, O house of Jacob, all you who remain of the house of Israel, you whom I have upheld since you were conceived, and have carried since your birth. Even to your old age and grey hairs I am he, I am he who will sustain you.

I have made you and I will carry you; I will sustain you and I will rescue you. Isaiah 46:4

Retirement seems such a moment of change that it is very easy to think that spiritual life also finishes at sixty or sixty-five – as if God is saying that there is no more to be done, we have come to an end. But these are *our* thoughts, certainly not his. Because our physical frame becomes weaker it does not mean that he abandons us. Is he conscious, one wonders, of age? Surely only inasmuch as he understands our concern, or the disabilities that it can bring. It is an encouragement to remember that it is the inner spiritual relationship with which he is concerned, and he will still be teaching and guiding us right to our last moments on earth. He will still be 'perfecting' us whatever age we reach, and he will not become impatient with us because the years mount up behind us.

Thank you for your love, that does not change – your understanding of us in every part of life, and the realization that you never withdraw from us as we grow old.

*

My heart rejoices in the Lord. 1 Samuel 2:1

If we claim to be without sin, we deceive ourselves and the truth is not in us. If we confess our sins, he is faithful and just and will forgive us our sins and purify us from all unrighteousness. 1 John 1:8–9

It is abundantly clear that no man lives free from guilt. Guilt is universal. But according as it is repressed or recognized, so it sets in motion one of two contradictory processes. Repressed it leads to anger, rebellion, fear and anxiety, a deadening of conscience, an increasing inability to recognize one's faults and a growing dominance of aggressive tendencies. But consciously recognized, it leads to repentance, to the peace and security of divine pardon, and in that way to a progressive refinement of conscience and a steady weakening of aggressive impulses.

Paul Tournier, *Guilt and Grace*

Keep my conscience sensitive, O Lord, that I may not grieve you by wrong thoughts or deeds.

*

The Lord your God is with you, he is mighty to save. Zephaniah 3:17

Then I saw a new heaven and a new earth, for the first heaven and the first earth had passed away, and there was no longer any sea. Revelation 21:1

The Christian hope is not that we will be taken up into some ethereal realm called 'heaven' but that we will live on the new earth with God. If the word 'heaven' really means the presence of God, this means that we will enjoy heaven on the earth. Our hope is not for redemption from the world, but for the redemption of the world. God will re-create all things and make them perfect as he did in the beginning.

David Watson, *Jesus Then and Now*

One day as your children we shall live in a new way with you, Father. All the things that cause tears, pain and sorrow will have gone. Thank you for the wonder and joy of all that you have prepared for us.

The Joy of the Lord

Praise and Thanks to You,
my Father and my God

Praise be to the Lord for ever! Psalm 89:52

For God was pleased to have all his fullness dwell in him, and through him to reconcile to himself all things, whether things on earth or things in heaven, by making peace through his blood, shed on the cross. Colossians 1:19–20

Have you felt there is no comfort? Remember Jesus Christ crucified. His crucifixion reveals a suffering God, who cares, who is *for* you, who feels with you. Have you felt there is no hope? Remember Jesus Christ raised from the dead. His resurrection reveals a conquering God, who will bring you through pain, sorrow and death itself to a new life in which the problem of suffering will be solved and perfect happiness and wholeness will be realized.

Charles Ohlrich, *The Suffering God*

Thank you, Father, for Christ my Saviour and for all that he has accomplished that I might journey through this life in the power of the resurrection journey until the day when my life on earth is finished and I begin a new life in heaven.

*

The Joy of the Lord

Praise the Lord, all his works everywhere in his dominion.
Psalm 103:22

Therefore, my dear friends, as you have always obeyed –
not only in my presence, but now much more in my absence
– continue to work out your salvation with fear and trembling, for it is God who works in you to will and to act
according to his good purpose. Philippians 2:12–13

Perhaps the greatest anguish that we go through as human
beings is that to be found through the mind. Rejection
brings a turmoil of emotions that becomes agony. Jealousy
is as poignant as the stab of a wound. A sense of inferiority
can make us feel as if we are struggling to breathe. We
sometimes make grave errors that rebound on others,
changing their lives and bringing them pain. Eventually,
because of these things, we begin to hate ourselves, we see
ourselves as worthless, nothing. It is only then, as we learn
about ourselves and accept what we see, a creature made by
and loved by the God who is ready to forgive and waiting to
work in us and to change us, that we shall be freed.

Thank you, Father, for the knowledge that you will not
abandon me, that your Spirit works in me. Cause me to
learn your lessons well, that I may grow spiritually according to your purpose.

*

123

Clap your hands, all you nations; shout to God with cries of joy. Psalm 47:1

If you obey my commands, you will remain in my love, just as I have obeyed my Father's commands and remain in his love. I have told you this so that my joy may be in you and that your joy may be complete. John 15:10–11

Life is not easy, clouds as well as sunshine come to us all. Our Lord here was facing the cross, with the scoffing, ill-treatment and rejection that came before it. Yet he spoke to his disciples of his joy being theirs, so that their joy might be complete. Nothing but his indwelling joy would keep them through all the trials that lay ahead. Nothing, and no one, could destroy that joy, not even martyrdom. It was in prison that Paul and Silas sang hymns of praise and thanksgiving when they knew not what the next day might hold for them.

Jean Coggan, *Welcome Life!*

I bring you my praise, thanking you for the joy of knowing you.

*

Great is the Lord, and most worthy of praise. Psalm 48:1

Come, let us sing for joy to the Lord: let us shout aloud to the Rock of our Salvation. Let us come before him with thanksgiving and extol him with music and song. . . . Come, let us bow down in worship, let us kneel before the Lord our

Maker; for he is our God and we are the people of his
pasture, the flock under his care. Psalm 95:1–2, 6–7

God calls for worship that involves our whole being. The
body, mind, spirit and emotions should all be laid on the
altar of worship.

Often we have forgotten that worship should include the
body as well as the mind and spirit.

The Bible describes worship in physical terms. The root
meaning for the Hebrew word we translate 'worship' is 'to
prostrate'. The word 'bless' literally means 'to kneel'.
Thanksgiving refers to 'an extension of the hand'. Throughout Scripture we find a variety of physical postures in
connection with worship; lying prostrate, standing, kneeling, lifting the hands, clapping the hands, lifting the head,
bowing the head, dancing and wearing sackcloth and ashes.
The point is that we are to offer God our bodies as well as all
the rest of our being. Worship is appropriately physical.

We are to present our bodies to God in worship in a
posture consistent with the inner spirit in worship. Standing, clapping, dancing, lifting the hands, lifting the head are
postures consistent with the spirit of praise. Kneeling, bowing the head, lying prostrate are postures consistent with the
spirit of humility.

Richard Foster, *Celebration of Discipline*

Praise you, Father, Alleluia.
Thank you for your love. Forgive me my sins – my
    unbelief.
Enable me to be more faithful – to give you pleasure.
Praise you – Alleluia.

*

Moments With God

Praise the Lord, for the Lord is good. Psalm 135:3

May the God of hope fill you with all joy and peace as you trust in him, so that you may overflow with hope by the power of the Holy Spirit. Romans 15:13

Joy is one of the fruits of the Spirit promised us. Yet perhaps some of us have misunderstood this word. We may think of joy as the exhilaration of prayers being miraculously answered: of the happiness of life going smoothly because of God's blessing on it; or the emotional euphoria of the singing and rejoicing of God's people in invigorating fellowship.

While God often graciously grants us these blessings, the joy of the Spirit is something deeper. The promise is not that the Christian will have only joyous circumstances, but that the Helper will give us the supernatural gift of joy in whatever circumstances we have.

It is his own joy that is pledged us. Through the Spirit, the risen and glorified Lord will himself take up residence in our cold hearts, and along with him comes his joy.

Catherine Marshall, *The Helper*

Joy is the certainty of the knowledge that Jesus is with me. Help me to hold to this assurance in moments when I feel bereft of human joy. Father, may I allow the Holy Spirit to work in me so that the fruit which comes from his presence may be seen, and glorify you.

*

Glory in his holy name; let the hearts of those who seek the Lord rejoice. Psalm 105:3

For I was hungry and you gave me something to eat, I was thirsty and you gave me something to drink, I was a stranger and you invited me in, I needed clothes and you clothed me, I was sick and you looked after me, I was in prison and you came to visit me. Matthew 25:35–36

How precious are the presents that children give, even though it may be the parent who is asked for the money with which to provide them. But the gift is no less acceptable.

Everything that we have comes from God. When we seek to give to him we only give what is already his. This does not make the gift unacceptable. On the contrary, the giving back enhances the gift. Our money, time, talents are all gifts from him; as we consciously return them it not only gives him pleasure but forges new links of love in our relationship.

Thank you for all that I have from you. Show me how to give to you – of my time, money, talents. Keep me from cheating you of any of these things.

*

Great is the Lord and most worthy of praise. Psalm 96:4

Be joyful always, pray continually; give thanks in all circumstances, for this is God's will for you in Christ Jesus. 1
Thessalonians 5:16

Our Father in heaven, hallowed be your name. Matthew 6:9

We are so self-centred that our thoughts naturally revolve
around ourselves and our own affairs. We then use prayer
merely to find quick relief from whatever is the problem of
the moment. On a human level we feel let down and sad if
people only want us to supply a need, and the more we love
the greater is the hurt. When Jesus taught his disciples the
form of prayer, acknowledgement of who was being approached and adoration came first. We do not come to God
for handouts but because of a relationship. The first thing to
do in prayer is to acknowledge him and the place he holds in
our life, then to praise and worship. This must always come
first, because that is the way God wills it.

I worship you as God, my Father, bringing you my praise
and thanking you for your care. My joy comes from knowing you. May I have the strength to give you thanks in all
circumstances, remembering that you do not change, you
are always faithful.

*

The Lord is God, and he has made his light shine upon us.
Psalm 118:27

They killed him by hanging him on a tree, but God raised
him from the dead on the third day and caused him to be
seen. Acts 10:39–40

A Religious Information Centre in North Carolina had on
display in its window a large picture of the dead Christ in
the arms of his mother. An old Negro lady opened the
door and pushed her head round the corner.

'That Jesus dead in your window?'

'Yes.'

'He done be killed by the bad mans?'

'Yes.'

'Done dead and gone for ever, that poor Jesus done gone
and dead for ever, huh?'

'No, he rose again on Easter morning.'

'Rose again? You mean he live again? He rise from the
dead? He really truly rise from the dead?'

'Yes – you must have heard the story of the Resurrection
before.'

And with a broad smile, her face bubbling with joy, the
old lady said, 'Oh, I done heard it before. I guess I done
heard it a million times before. But I just glories to hear it
again.'

Jesus is alive, still, today. Jesus is God's gift to the
world, the Godsend for which Christians can never stop
being thankful.

H. J. Richards,
The First Christmas: What Really Happened?

Thank you for Christmas, when Jesus came on earth.
Thank you that at Easter, Jesus was willing to die for us.

Thank you for the glorious morning when Jesus rose again. Thank you that Jesus is alive.

*

Praise be to you, O Lord; teach me your decrees. Psalm 119:12

Glory in his holy name; let the hearts of those who seek the Lord rejoice. Look to the Lord and his strength; seek his face always. Psalm 105:3–4

We pray in order to be closer to God. I would prefer to put this differently and say: I want to put aside each day just a few minutes, so that God may draw closer to me. This already shows one important result of our praying. God is in touch with us, as friends can be in touch, making known to us what he wants of us. We begin to see sense, almost by instinct, what is pleasing to him and what is not.

Furthermore, we begin to understand things about him which we did not before. For instance, we may suddenly realize how much he wants us just from reading about our Lord's attitude to people in the Gospel. What was once just a story which might have been told by an acquaintance, becomes a personal message from one who is fast becoming a firm friend.

Again, the result of prayer will be to keep God and his will for us at the top of our priorities. We shall, too, be more sensitive to the needs of other people and be moved to do something to help. If we keep our eyes on God, we cannot fail to see the needs of our neighbour.

Wisdom and understanding are the fruits of prayer. We become clearer about the end to which we are travelling on life's pilgrimage, and more certain of the means to be adopted to get there. And however rough the going becomes, we have the courage to go on, remaining deep down in peace.

Basil Hume, OSB, *To Be a Pilgrim*

Father, I forget that you long for me. I think only of my own feelings. I want so to live my life with you, that I keep myself in your presence as naturally as I breathe.

*

I trust in you, O Lord; I say, 'You are my God.' Psalm 31:14

Let the peace of Christ rule in your hearts, since as members of one body you were called to peace. And be thankful. Colossians 3:15

The thankful heart brings a special bonus to the task of daily living. The habit of saying 'Thank you, Lord' when we open the door of the fridge reminds us that without it shopping and keeping food would be more difficult. Being thankful for a home, however small and mean, for bed and warmth, money to pay for the necessities of life, enables us to see that God has given us these things. If then we are tempted to think that we have to work for these then we may give thanks for the ability to do so. Being truly thankful works its own small miracle within the context of our spiritual life, quite apart from it being right and proper to acknowledge the Giver. Eventually it also helps to weaken that evil of resentment that attempts to smoulder on in our life when we feel that we do not have so much as others. By building on the things for which we are thankful we may well find that there seem to be more and more.

Open my eyes, Father, to your giving. I want to have a thankful heart that appreciates those good things that come into my life.

*

I am the Lord, who has made all things. Isaiah 44:24

Clap your hands, all you nations; shout to God with cries of joy. How awesome is the Lord Most High, the great King over all the earth! Psalm 47:1–2

It is very difficult for us today to recapture this zest of pure worship. One reason why it is difficult is that we seek to justify everything we do by tangible results for ourselves or others. We hear a church service praised because it 'made me feel good'. Acts of worship are turned into experiences of emotional togetherness which are valued for the personal boost they provide for individuals and groups. But anything which thrusts the purpose of worship back into conscious self-improvement is alien to that bouncing outgoingness represented by the psalmist's shouts of delight in the hill of Sion, the city of our God, the Lord our Governor, great in Sion, and high above all people.

Harry Blamires, *On Christian Truth*

I long to praise you in the way that brings glory to your name and truly pleases you. May your Holy Spirit teach me to do so in love, thankfulness and in utter unselfconsciousness.

*

Give thanks to the Lord of lords: his love endures for ever. Psalm 136:3

So then, just as you received Christ Jesus as Lord, continue to live in him, rooted and built up in him, strengthened in the faith as you were taught, and overflowing with thankfulness. Colossians 2:6–7

When we live thankfully, we praise God. Inevitably times will come when people say, 'How can you be so cheerful?', and the answer simply and sincerely will be, 'Well, I have so much for which to thank God'. It is not our circumstances which need to change so very often, but our attitude to them. When I live thankfully – whatever my lot – I praise God, for I am silently declaring that I believe God knows what is best for me, and I count his will as best.

Derek Prime, *Created to Praise*

I want to be an upward and outward looking person, Lord, with thankfulness in my heart and praise on my lips. Help me to remember your goodness at all times.

Acknowledgements

All biblical quotations are taken from the Holy Bible, New International Version, published in the USA by New York Bible Society and in Great Britain by Hodder & Stoughton.

For anyone who would like to read further, the texts quoted in the book come from the following sources:–

Bruce Milne, *The End of the World*, Kingsway Publications

Richard F. Lovelace, *Dynamics of Spiritual Life*, Paternoster Press

Stephen H. Travers, *I Believe in the Second Coming of Christ*, Hodder & Stoughton

Alan Durden, *Jesus Praise*, Scripture Union

Martin Israel, *The Pain that Heals*, Hodder & Stoughton

Paul Tournier, *The Adventure of Living*, Highland Books

Donald Coggan, *Convictions*, Hodder & Stoughton

Francis MacNutt, *The Healing Ministry*, Ave Maria Press

Carlo Carretto, *Letters From the Desert*, Darton, Longman & Todd

Paul E. Billheimer, *The Mystery of His Providence*, Kingsway Publications

William Barclay, *Jesus As They Saw Him*, SCM Press

Andrew Murray, *With Christ in the School of Prayer*, Lakeland Books

Helen Roseveare, *Living Faith*, Hodder & Stoughton

J. Neville Ward, *The Use of Praying*, Epworth Press

R. T. Kendall, *Once Saved, Always Saved*, Hodder & Stoughton

Acknowledgements

Norman Vincent Peale and Smiley Blanton, *Faith is the Answer*, World's Work

Florence Allshorn, *The Notebooks of Florence Allshorn*, SCM Press

Robert Runcie, *Windows Onto God*, SPCK

Leo Sherley Price, Introduction, *The Ladder of Perfection*, Penguin

David Hewetson and David Miller, *Christianity Made Simple*, Albatross

Andrew Murray, *The Best of Andrew Murray*, Kingsway Publications

Cardinal Basil Hume, OSB, *Searching for God*, Hodder & Stoughton

William Young Fullerton, *Baptist Hymnbook*, Carey Kingsgate Press

Anthony Bloom, *God and Man*, Darton, Longman & Todd

David Parry, *This Promise is for You*, Darton, Longman & Todd

Andrew Knowles, *Finding Faith*, Lion Publishing

Michael Green, *I Believe in Satan's Downfall*, Hodder & Stoughton

Alan Loy McGinnis, *The Friendship Factor*, Hodder & Stoughton

Charles R. Swindoll, *Strengthening Your Grip*, Hodder & Stoughton

Jutta Jarnagin, *The Raging*, Kingsway Publications

Faith Lees, *Break Open My World*, Marshall, Morgan & Scott

Jim Smith, *Time to Share*, Kingsway Publications

Lewis Smedes, *Mere Morality*, Lion Publishing

Fritz Ridenour, *How to be a Christian without being Religious*, Regal Books

Michael Baughen, *The Prayer Principle*, Mowbray

J. Neville Ward, *Five for Sorrow, Ten for Joy*, Epworth Press

Acknowledgements

Michel Quoist, *The Christian Response*, Gill & Macmillan

Léon Joseph, Cardinal Suenens, *A New Pentecost?*, Darton, Longman & Todd

Donald Bridge and David Phypers, *Growing in God's Family*, Hodder & Stoughton

Catherine Marshall, *A Man Called Peter*, Fount Paperbacks

Hanna Ahrens, *Who'd be a Mum!*, Lion Publishing

J. Oswald Sanders, *Paul the Leader*, Kingsway Publications

Mother Teresa, *The Love of Christ*, Fount Paperbacks

Gien Karssen, *Getting the Most out of Being Single*, Navigator Press

Roger Forster, *We Believe in Marriage*, Marshall, Morgan & Scott

Robert Llewelyn, *With Pity not with Blame*, Darton, Longman & Todd

John W. Stott, *Christian Counter Culture*, InterVarsity Press

Andrew Kirk, *A New World Coming*, Marshall, Morgan & Scott

Elizabeth Elliot, *Discipline – the Glad Surrender*, Pickering & Inglis

William Barclay, *Jesus As They Saw Him*, SCM Press

Billy Graham, *The Secret of Happiness*, World's Work

David Watson, *Is Anyone There?*, Hodder & Stoughton

John Woolmer, *Growing up to Salvation*, Triangle

David Sheppard, *Bias to the Poor*, Hodder & Stoughton

St Teresa of Avila, *A Life of Prayer*, Pickering & Inglis

Sheila Cassidy, *Prayer for Pilgrims*, Fount Paperbacks

Joni Eareckson and Steve Estes, *A Step Further*, Pickering & Inglis

Harold Bauman, *Living Through Grief*, Lion Publishing

Margaret Evening, *Who Walk Alone*, Hodder & Stoughton

Diana Peck, *Decision Magazine*, July/August 1983, Billy Graham Association

Julian of Norwich, *Enfolded in Love*, Darton, Longman & Todd

Edith Schaeffer, *Affliction*, Hodder & Stoughton

Reginald East, *Heal the Sick*, Hodder & Stoughton

Charles Swindoll, *Three Steps Forward, Two Steps Back*, Pickering & Inglis

W. E. Sangster, *The Secret of a Radiant Life*, Hodder & Stoughton

Noreen Riols, *Eye of the Storm*, Hodder & Stoughton

M. David Enoch, *Healing the Hurt Mind*, Hodder & Stoughton

Jane Davies, *The Price of Loving*, Mowbray

Carol Oldham, *A Child Loaned*, Kingsway Publications

Hannah Pearsall Smith, *The Christians' Secret of a Happy Life*, Marshall, Morgan & Scott

Charles Swindoll, *Strike the Original Match*, Kingsway Publications

H. A. Williams, *The True Wilderness*, Fount Paperbacks

J. Oswald Sanders, *Effective Evangelism*, Send the Light Trust

G. A. Studdert Kennedy, *The Unutterable Beauty*, Mowbray

J. B. Phillips, *Through the Year with J. B. Phillips*, Arthur James

John White, *The Golden Cow*, Marshall, Morgan & Scott

Frank Topping, *The Words of Christ*, Lutterworth Press

Stuart Briscoe, *Bound for Joy*, Regal Books

Martin Israel, *Smouldering Fire*, Hodder & Stoughton

Paul Tournier, *Guilt and Grace*, Hodder & Stoughton

David Watson, *Jesus Then and Now*, Lion Publishing

Charles Ohlrich, *The Suffering God*, Triangle

Jean Coggan, *Welcome Life!*, Mowbray

Richard Foster, *Celebration of Discipline*, Hodder & Stoughton

Catherine Marshall, *The Helper*, Hodder & Stoughton

Acknowledgements

H. J. Richards, *The First Christmas: What Really Happened?*, Mowbray

Cardinal Basil Hume, OSB, *To Be a Pilgrim*, St Paul Publications/SPCK

Harry Blamires, *On Christian Truth*, SPCK

Derek Prime, *Created to Praise*, Hodder & Stoughton

Also available in Fount Paperbacks

The Holy Spirit
BILLY GRAHAM

'This is far and away Graham's best book. It bears the stamp of someone who has seen everything, and then has worked painstakingly and carefully in making his own assessment . . . The Christian world will be reading it for many years to come.'

Richard Bewes,
Church of England Newspaper

To Live Again
CATHERINE MARSHALL

The moving story of one woman's heart-rending grief and of her long hard struggle to rediscovery of herself, of life, of hope.

A Man Called Peter
CATHERINE MARSHALL

The story of a brilliantly successful minister and of a dynamic personality. Told by his wife, it is also the story of their life together; a record of love and faith that has few equals in real life.

The Prayers of Peter Marshall
CATHERINE MARSHALL

'This is a truly wonderful book, for these prayers are a man speaking to God – and speaking in a way that involves listening for an answer.'

British Weekly

Also available in Fount Paperbacks

BOOKS BY C. S. LEWIS

Reflections on the Psalms

'Absolutely packed with wisdom. It is clearly the fruit of very much reflection . . . upon one's own darkness of spirit, one's own fumbling and grasping in the shadows of prayer or of penitence.'

Trevor Huddleston

Miracles

'This is a brilliant book, abounding in lucid exposition and illuminating metaphor.'

Charles Davey, The Observer

The Problem of Pain

'Written with clarity and force, and out of much knowledge and experience.'

Times Literary Supplement

Surprised by Joy

'His outstanding gift is clarity. You can take it at two levels, as straight autobiography, or as a kind of spiritual thriller, a detective's probing of clue and motive . . .'

Isabel Quigley, Sunday Times

Also available in Fount Paperbacks

A Gift for God
MOTHER TERESA OF CALCUTTA

'The force of her words is very great . . . the message is always the same, yet always fresh and striking.'

Malcolm Muggeridge

Strength to Love
MARTIN LUTHER KING

'The sermons . . . read easily and reveal a man of great purpose, humility and wisdom . . . in the turbulent context of the American race conflict, Dr King's statements have the ring of social as well as spiritual truth . . .'

Steven Kroll
The Listener

A Book of Comfort
ELIZABETH GOUDGE ·

'The contents are worth ten of the title: this is a careful, sensitive anthology of the illuminations in prose and verse that have prevented the world from going wholly dark over the centuries.'

Sunday Times

The Desert in the City
CARLO CARRETTO

'. . . we have been in the hands of one of the finest of modern spiritual writers, who helps us on the road of love in Christ.'

Philip Cauvin, the Universe

Also available in Fount Paperbacks

Audacity to Believe
SHEILA CASSIDY

'A story of extraordinarily unpretentious courage in the horror of Chile after Allende's overthrow. It is easy to read, totally sincere and sometimes moving. Sheila Cassidy is totally disarming.'

Frank O'Reilly
The Furrow

Prayer for Pilgrims
SHEILA CASSIDY

'. . . a direct and practical book about prayer . . . has the freshness of someone who writes of what she has personally discovered . . . many people . . . will be grateful for this book and helped by it.'

Neville Ward
Church Times

The General Next to God
RICHARD COLLIER

'An absorbing, sympathetic record of the man (General Booth) and his family and the movement they created.'

Michael Foot
Evening Standard

Fount Paperbacks

Fount is one of the leading paperback publishers of religious books and below are some of its recent titles.

- ☐ THE QUIET HEART George Appleton £2.95
- ☐ PRAYER FOR ALL TIMES Pierre Charles £1.75
- ☐ SEEKING GOD Esther de Waal £1.75
- ☐ THE SCARLET AND THE BLACK
  J. P. Gallagher £1.75
- ☐ TELL MY PEOPLE I LOVE THEM
  Clifford Hill £1.50
- ☐ CONVERSATIONS WITH THE CRUCIFIED
  Reid Isaac £1.50
- ☐ THE LITTLE BOOK OF SYLVANUS
  David Kossoff £1.50
- ☐ DOES GOD EXIST? Hans Küng £5.95
- ☐ GEORGE MACDONALD: AN ANTHOLOGY
  George MacDonald C. S. Lewis (ed.) £1.50
- ☐ WHY I AM STILL A CATHOLIC
  Robert Nowell (ed.) £1.50
- ☐ THE GOSPEL FROM OUTER SPACE
  Robert L. Short £1.50
- ☐ CONTINUALLY AWARE Rita Snowden £1.75
- ☐ TRUE RESURRECTION Harry Williams £1.75
- ☐ WHO WILL DELIVER US? Paul Zahl £1.50

All Fount paperbacks are available at your bookshop or newsagent, or they can also be ordered by post from Fount Paperbacks, Cash Sales Department, G.P.O. Box 29, Douglas, Isle of Man, British Isles. Please send purchase price, plus 15p per book, maximum postage £3. Customers outside the U.K. send purchase price, plus 15p per book. Cheque, postal or money order. No currency.

NAME (Block letters) _____

ADDRESS _____

_____

_____

While every effort is made to keep prices low, it is sometimes necessary to increase them at short notice. Fount Paperbacks reserve the right to show new retail prices on covers which may differ from those previously advertised in the text or elsewhere.